English 1

ACTIVITY

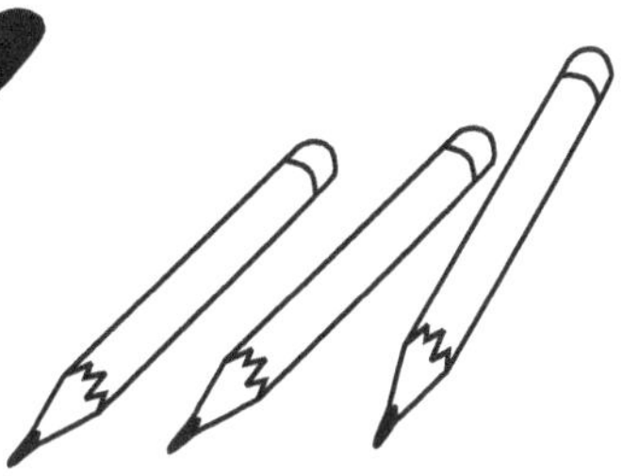

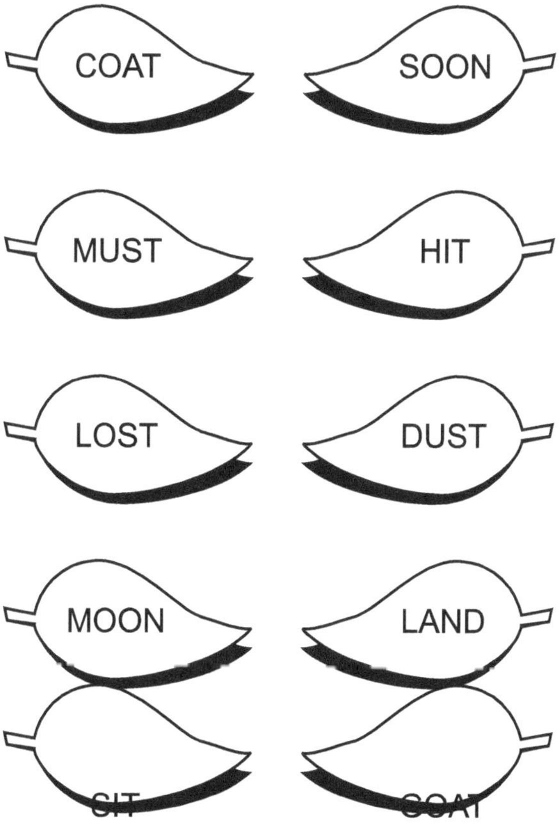

MANOJ PUBLICATIONS

The days of the children are full of activities. While awake they never sit idle. Activities and children are complementary to each other. This specially designed Jumbo Activity Book is full of participative creative drawings, that include fill the blanks, match the pictures, jumble words, puzzles, mazes, colouring etc. Working with this book will be a real fun for children. It is not only interesting & entertaining but also helpful in improving natural creative power of the children. This book will also help stimulate the child's reasoning power. Those who want to mould their children's activities in a positive and creative pattern, this book should prove a great help.

A Healthy & Happy Recreation for Tender Hearts.

-Publishers

Jumbo English Activity Book - 1

Publisher:

MANOJ PUBLICATIONS

761, Main Road, Burari, Delhi-110084
Mob. :   09999476076, 9868112194,
             8178823569, 8178854810
Email: info@manojpublications.com

For online shopping visit our website:
www.sawanonlinebookstore.com

ISBN : 978-81-310-0887-4

Printed by:
Jai Maya Offset
Delhi

Can you write your schedule for the entire day? And colour the picture.

Hi! I am Toto

I get up at 6'O clock in the morning.

My name is Emma. Identify my family members.

Grandfather	Father	Uncle	Mother
Sister	Brother	Grandmother	Aunt

It's me, Emma

....

....

....

....

....

....

....

....

Jumbo English Activity-1

Write the alphabet from A to Z in the boxes and colour them.

Liam wants to cross the river by stopping on the alphabetical stones from A to I. Help him by colouring the picture to highlight the stones.

In the crossword puzzle given below the names of the relatives are incomplete.
Complete the crossword.

Change the first letter of each word to 'W 'and write the new word in the blank blurb.

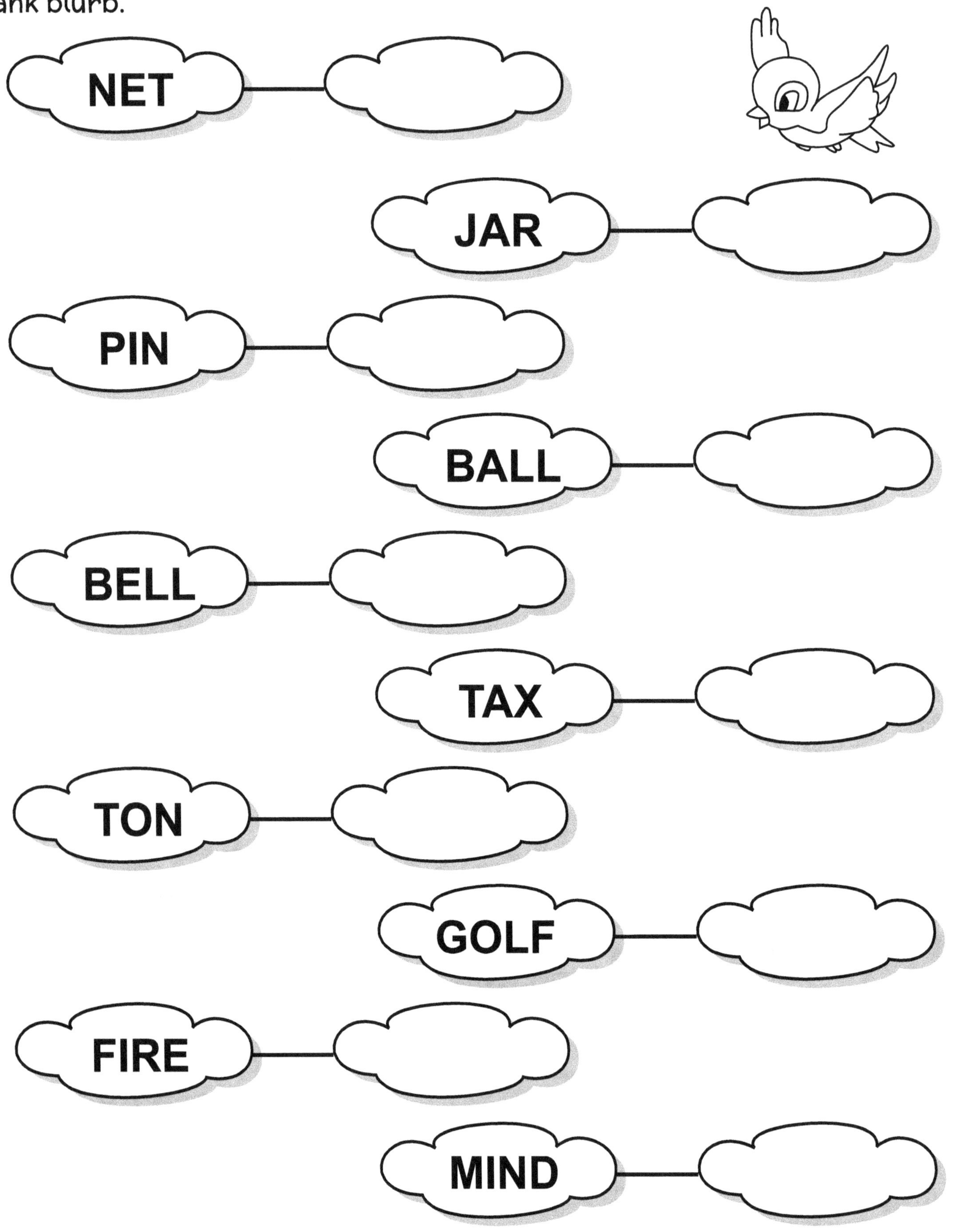

Jumbo English Activity-1

Complete the words by filling in the missing letters and colour the pictures.

M __ON

E __ G

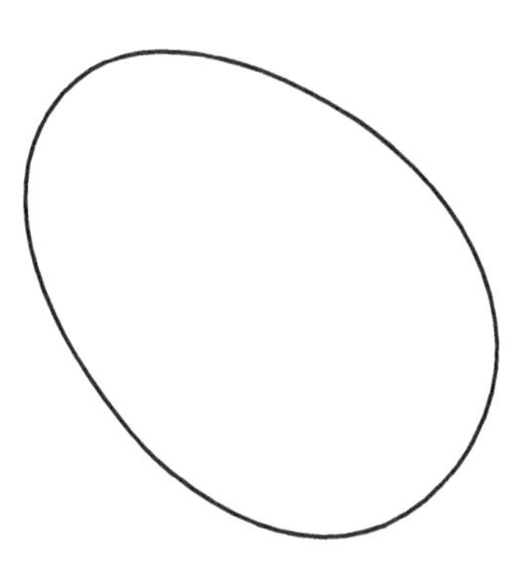

DU __ K

S __ UIRR __ L

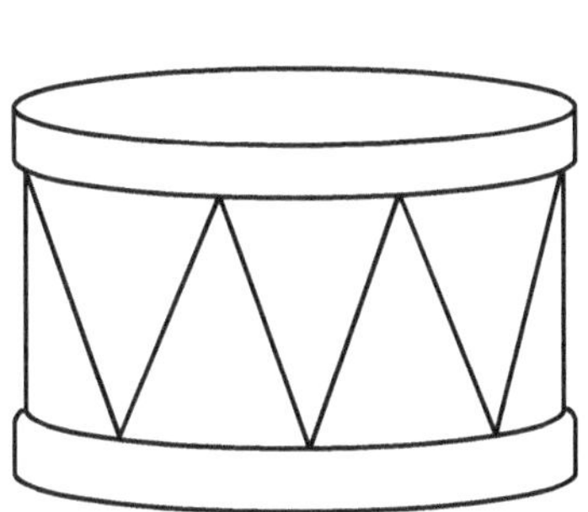

D __ UM

AER __ PLA __ E

C __ W

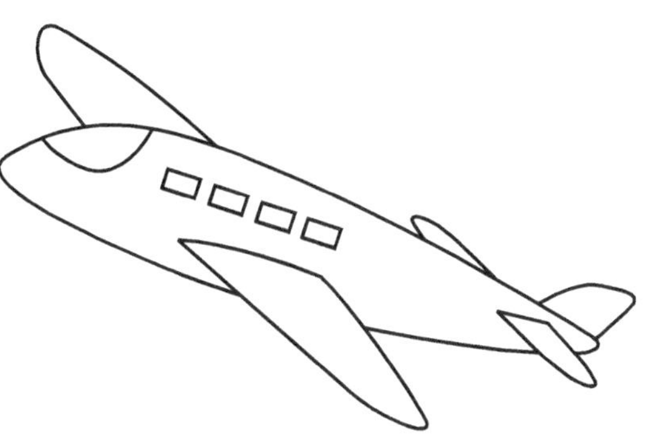

RA __ B __ T

T __ B __ E

Look at the pictures carefully. Do they end with the same sound? For yes colour 'Yes box'green and for no colour 'No box' in red.

| Yes | No |

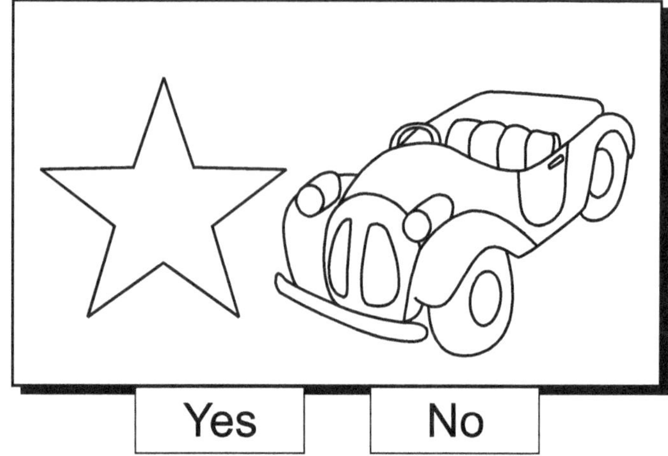

| Yes | No |

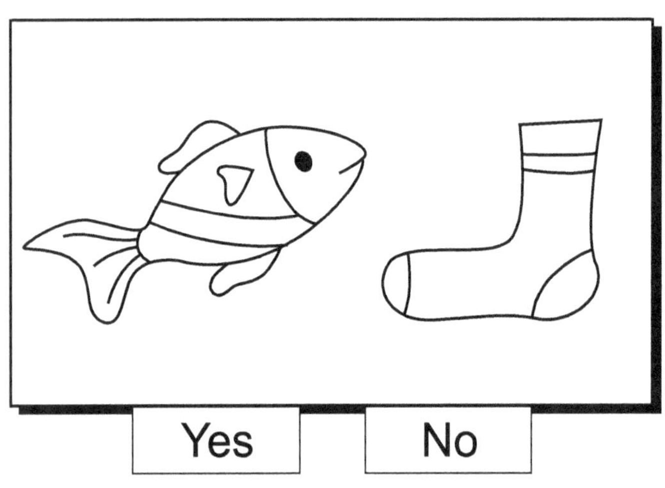

| Yes | No |

| Yes | No |

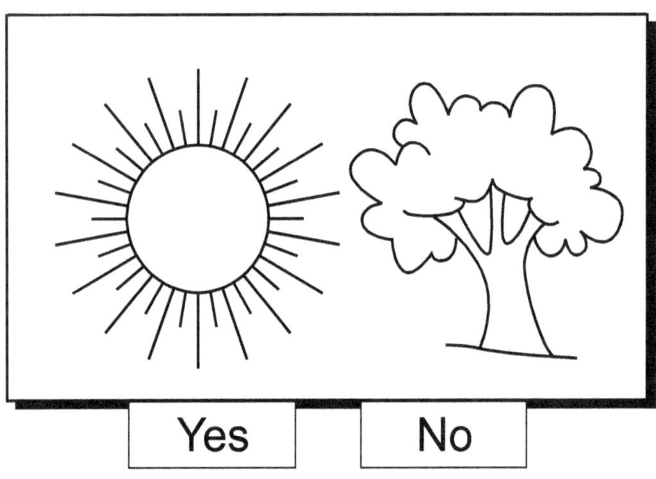

| Yes | No |

| Yes | No |

Jumbo English Activity-1

See the pictures and (×) mark in front of wrong answers.

Eating food ☐
Cooking food ☐

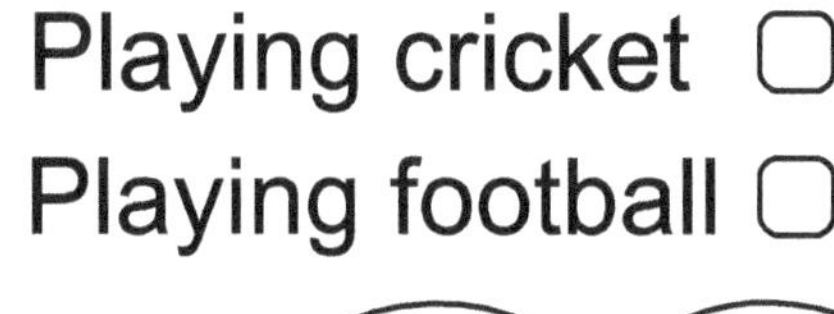

Barking ☐
Yawning ☐

Colour as many beads in the string as the number written below each row.

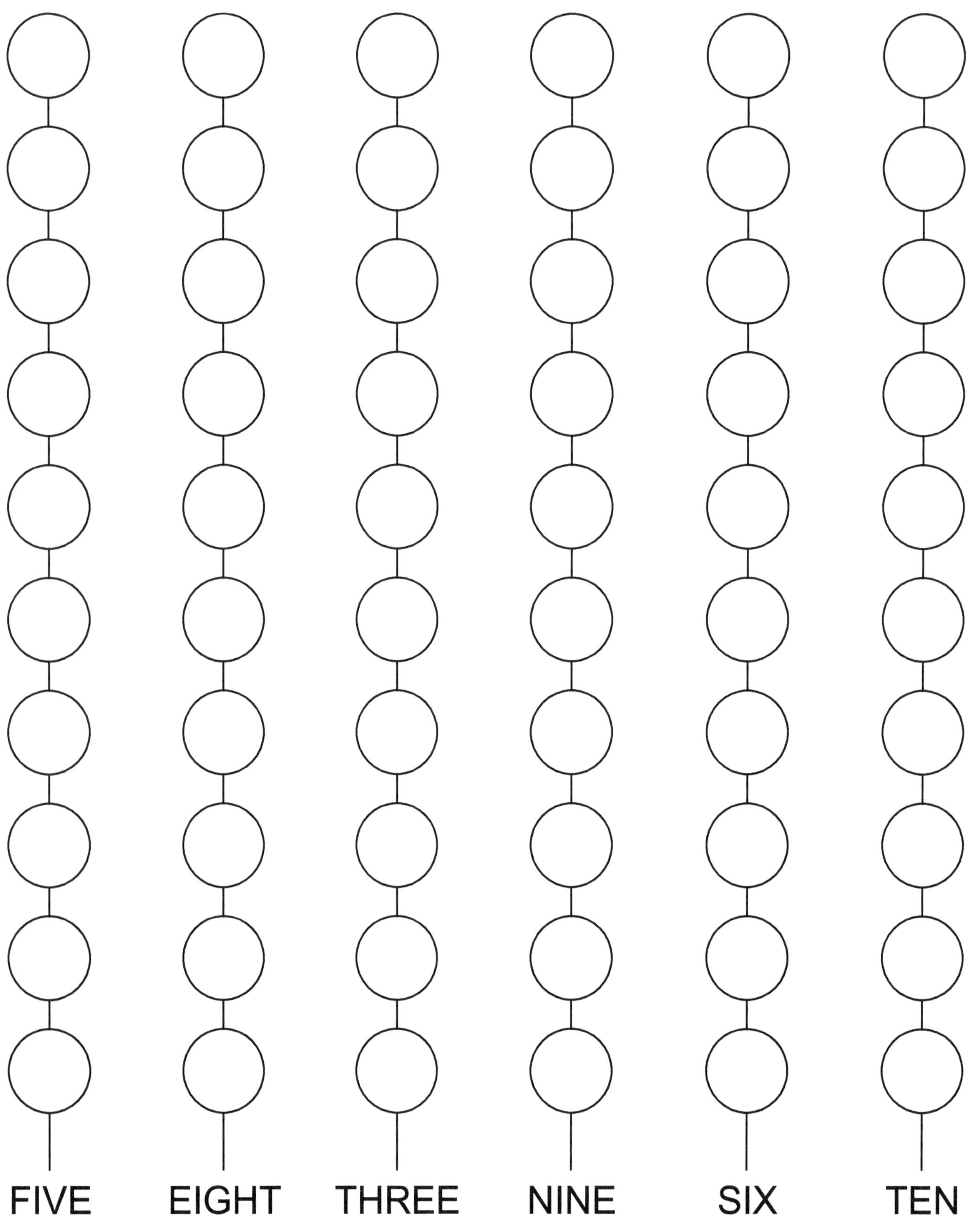

Jumbo English Activity–1

Connect three pictures with a straight line across, vertically or diagonally that start with the same letter and colour them.

Write small letter or capital letter as required in circles. Follow the example of 'A a' for guidance.

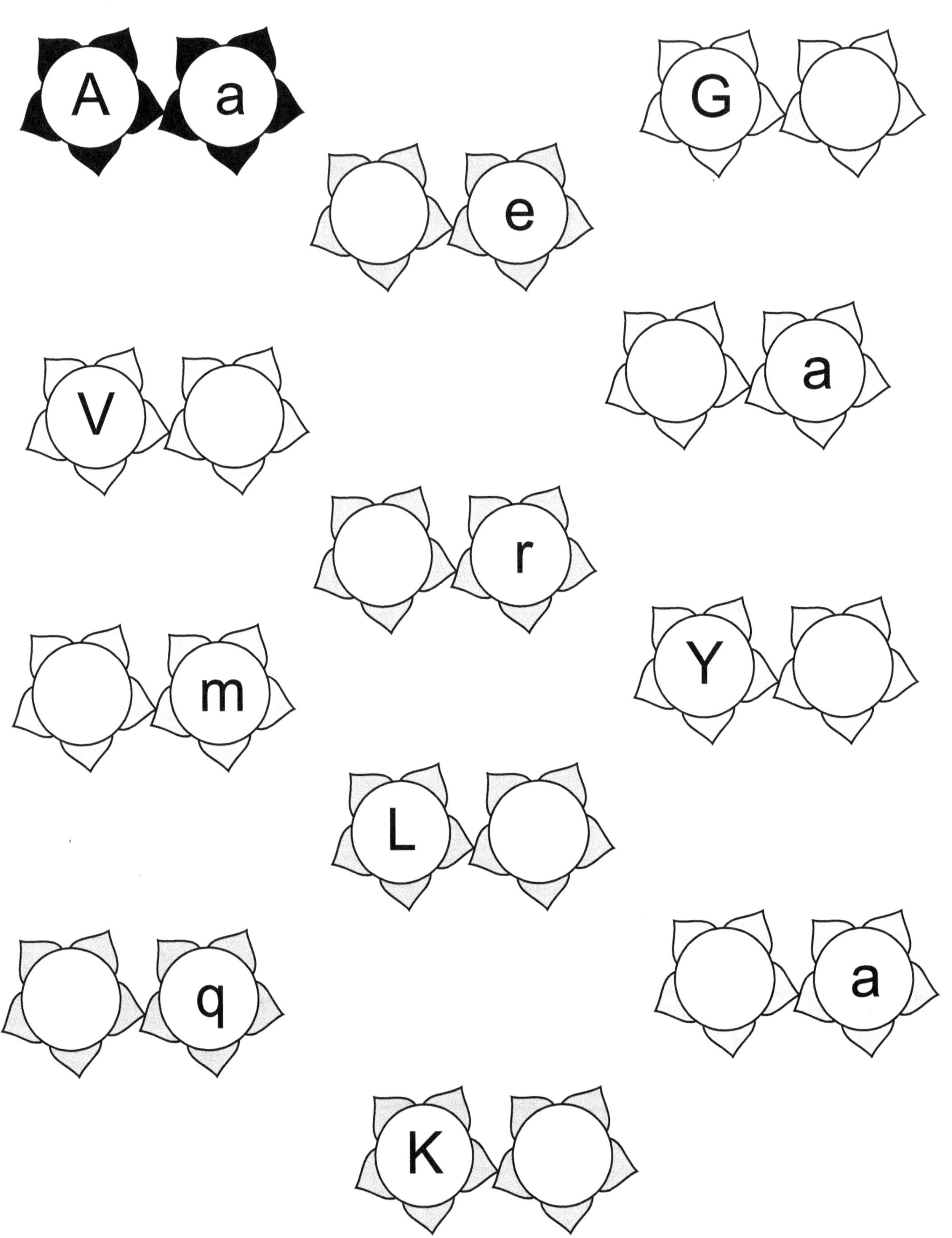

Match the pictures with correct words. Show it with arrows.

See the picture carefully and mark the answers in (✓) or (✗) in blank boxes.

1. Father is telling a story to the boy. ☐

2. Dog is lapping milk. ☐

3. There is an empty glass on the table. ☐

4. There are six stars with the moon. ☐

5. The father has a beard. ☐

6. It is not a full moon night. ☐

7. The boy is crying. ☐

8. The window curtains are plain. ☐

9. The father wears striped night dress. ☐

Abbreviation is the short form of a word. Write the abbreviations for the months of a year. An example is given below on the top.

January	Jan.
February	__________
March	__________
April	__________
May	__________
June	__________
July	__________
August	__________
September	__________
October	__________
November	__________
December	__________

Write the letters in the alphabetical order. See the example.

a b c d e f g h i j k l m n o p q r s t u v w x y z

1.	e	f	c	1.	e	c	f
2.	a	d	b	2.			
3.	x	z	y	3.			
4.	b	k	g	4.			
5.	m	o	a	5.			
6.	i	h	k	6.			
7.	l	m	s	7.			
8.	u	m	v	8.			
9.	u	s	t	9.			
10.	w	v	u	10.			

Jumbo English Activity-1

Fill in the blanks taking help of the key words provided at the bottom.

Humpty Dumpty sat on a _______

Humpty Dumpty had a_______fall

All the king's _______

And all the _______ men

Couldn't put Humpty_______

_________ again

KEY WORDS		
king's	great	together
horses	wall	Dumpty

Eight different caps for 8 different people. Match who wears which?

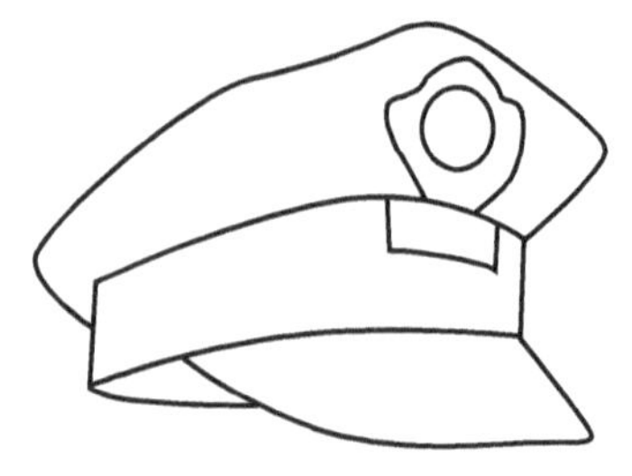

Clown

Witch

Police Officer

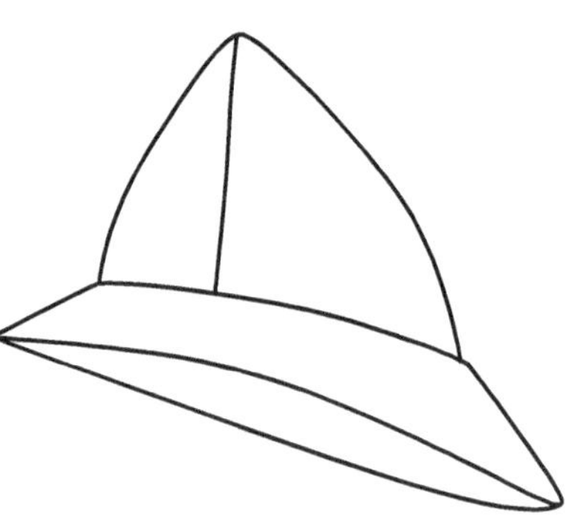

Fireman

Chef

Cowboy

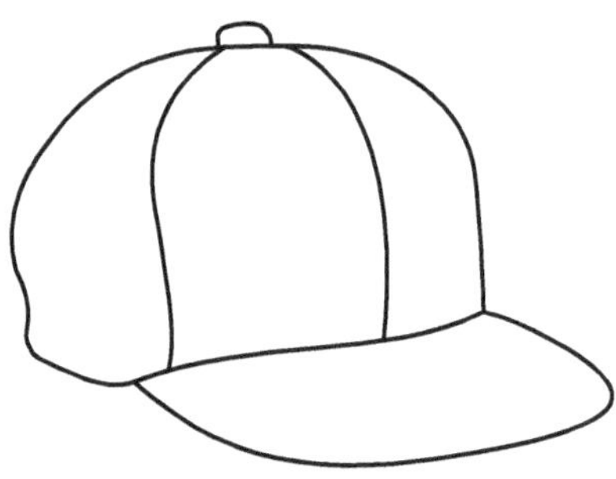

Sailer

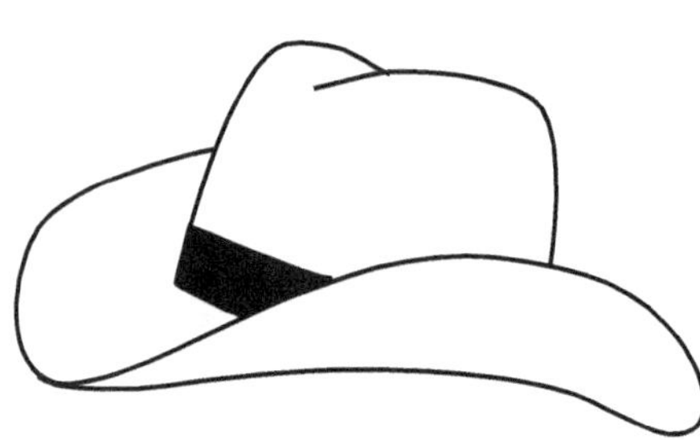

Cricketer

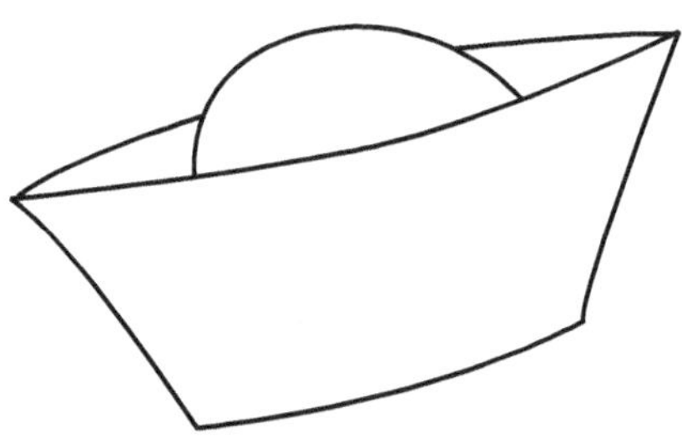

Draw a line to the sentence that relates to the picture.

Digging the earth

In the Garden

Sleeping

Going to school

In a jolly mood

Flying

Look at the pictures and write the correct word in the blank of each sentence.

1. 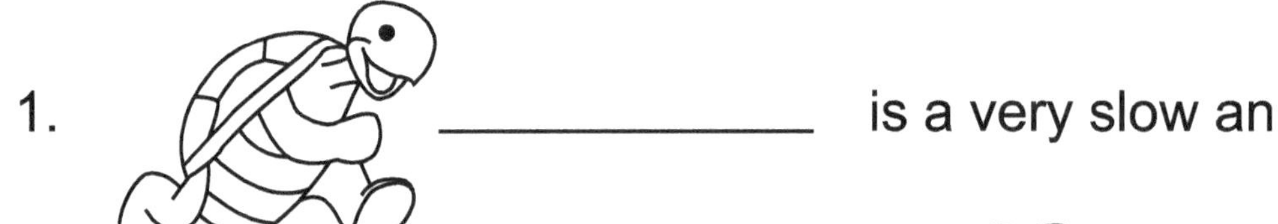 __________ is a very slow animal.

2. As wise as an ________ 

3. ________ is a farm bird.

4. An ________  a day keeps the doctor away.

5. 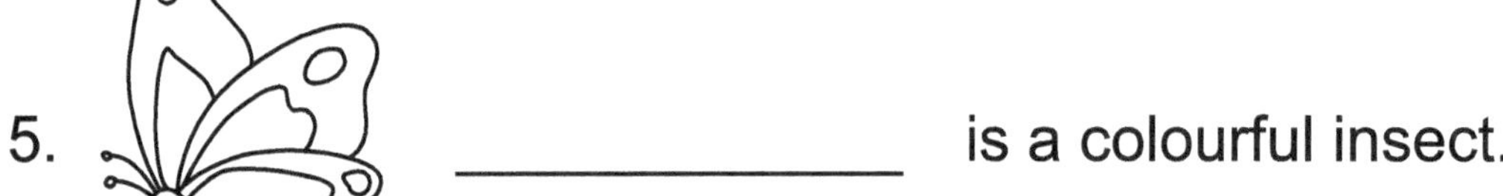 __________ is a colourful insect.

6. There is a ________  in the pond.

7. I live in my ________  with my family.

8. He is playing with __________ 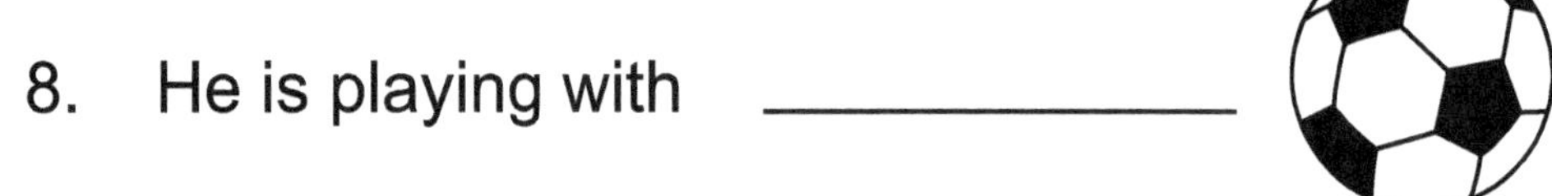

Match the sounds with the pictures.

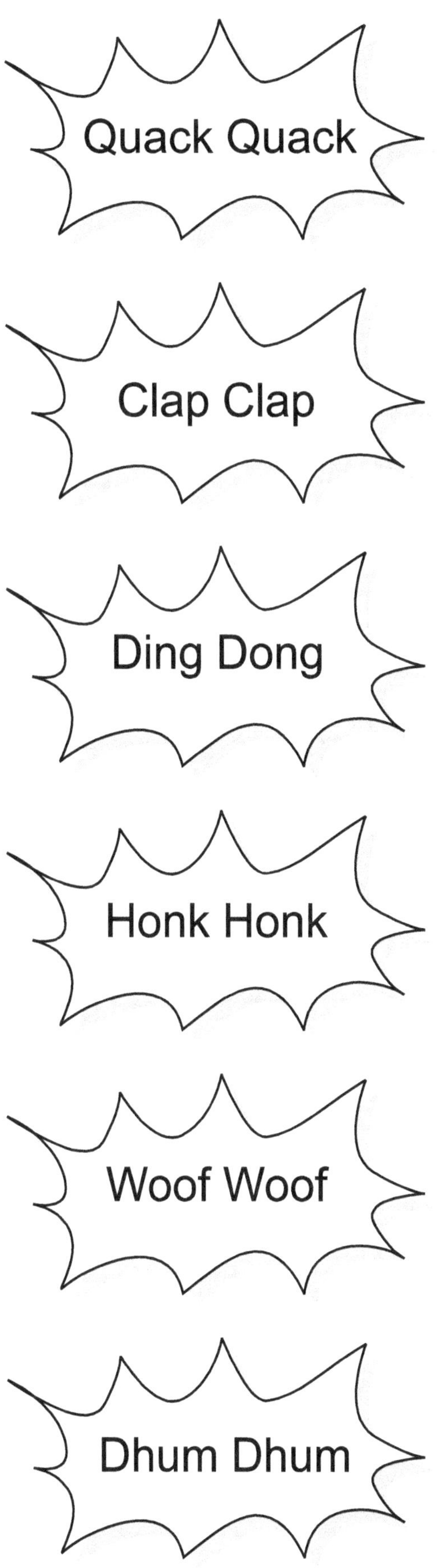

Look at the pictures carefully and fill in the blanks.

1. The .... likes to eat ....

2. The .... lives in a ....

3. There is a .... under the ....

4. The .... likes to eat ....

5. The .... is playing ....

Jumbo English Activity-1

Sam has different moods. With the help of the key words given at bottom choose the correct word for each box.

• Happy   • Sad   • Angry   • Pleased   • Sleepy   • Confused

Young teacher has written a few words for naughty Lucas in code language.
Help Pappu decode them and write it in the blanks.

Ω=A   Ψ=D   ♣=E   ∅=F   ∉=H   ∇=I   ⊆=M   ∈=N
⊄=O   ∪=R   ⊗=S   ⊕=T   ϖ=U   φ=W   ⊖=Y

Objects in singular form are to your left. Make them plurals to match the objects to your right.

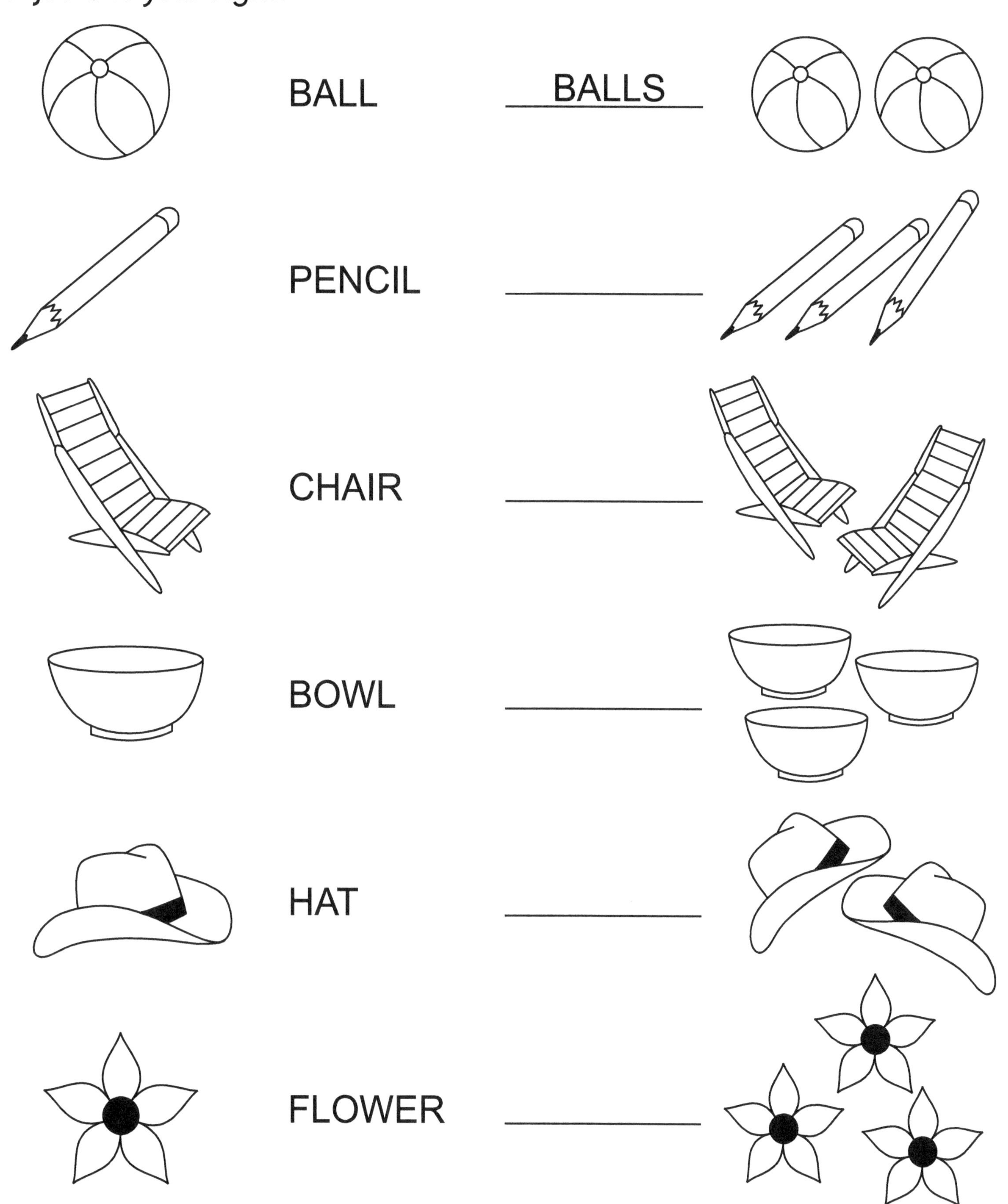

BALL   <u>BALLS</u>

PENCIL   _______

CHAIR   _______

BOWL   _______

HAT   _______

FLOWER   _______

Fill in the blanks to complete the poem and colour the picture.

Johny, Johny, _______________

Eating sugar, ______________

Telling lies, ______________

Open your mouth, ______________

Draw a line to the each similar sounding word that rhymes.

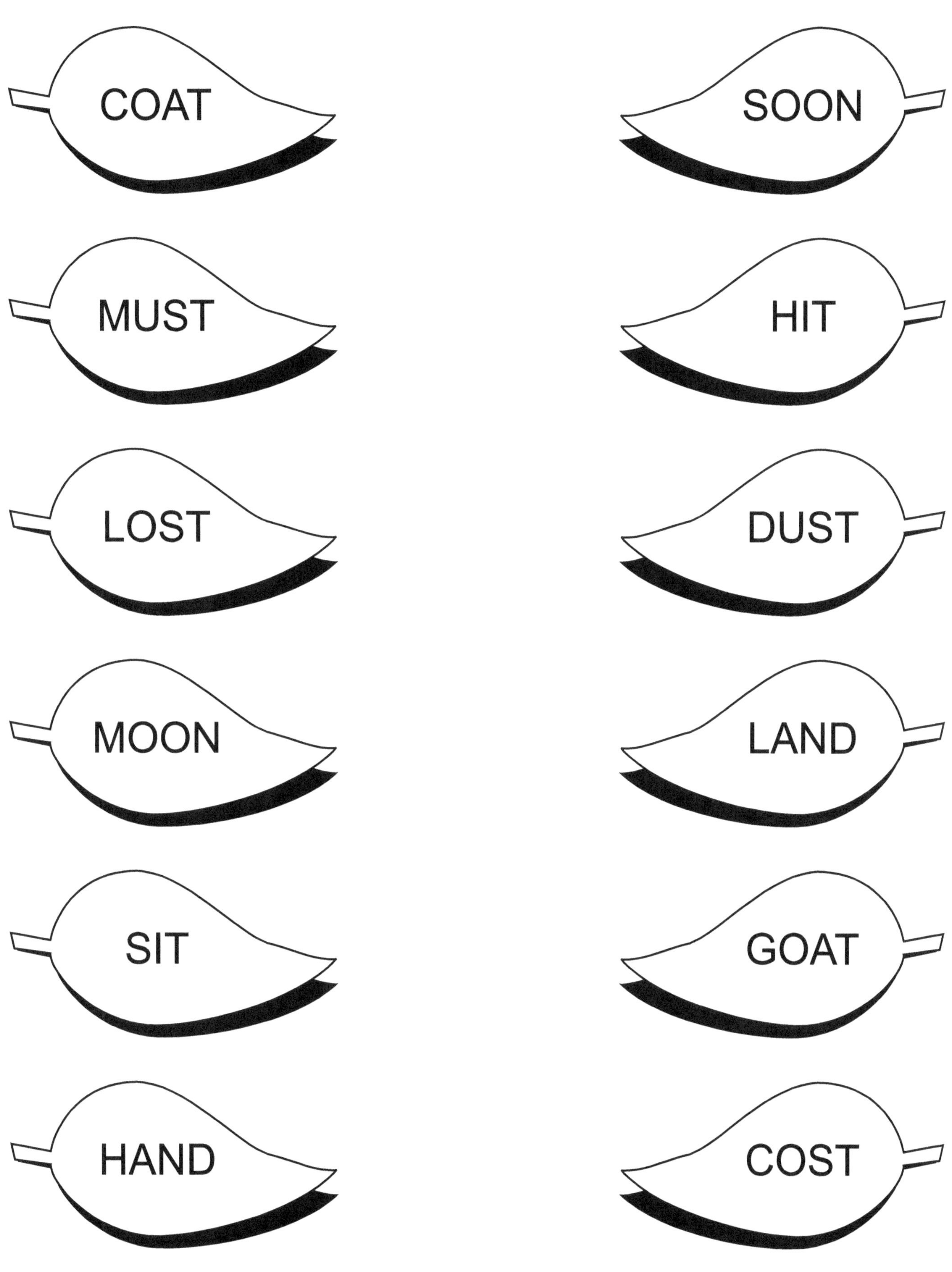

Sophia is searching for things which begin with 'S'. Colour them to make her task easy. Also write their names in the blanks below.

....

....

....

Jumbo English Activity-1

Change the first letter of each word to 'L' to get the new word.

MAP → LAP

TICK _______

MINE _______

FIGHT _______

DATE _______

SET _______

BETTER _______

COCK _______

Identify the names of that are pictured below. Cross out the wrong one and colour the right one.

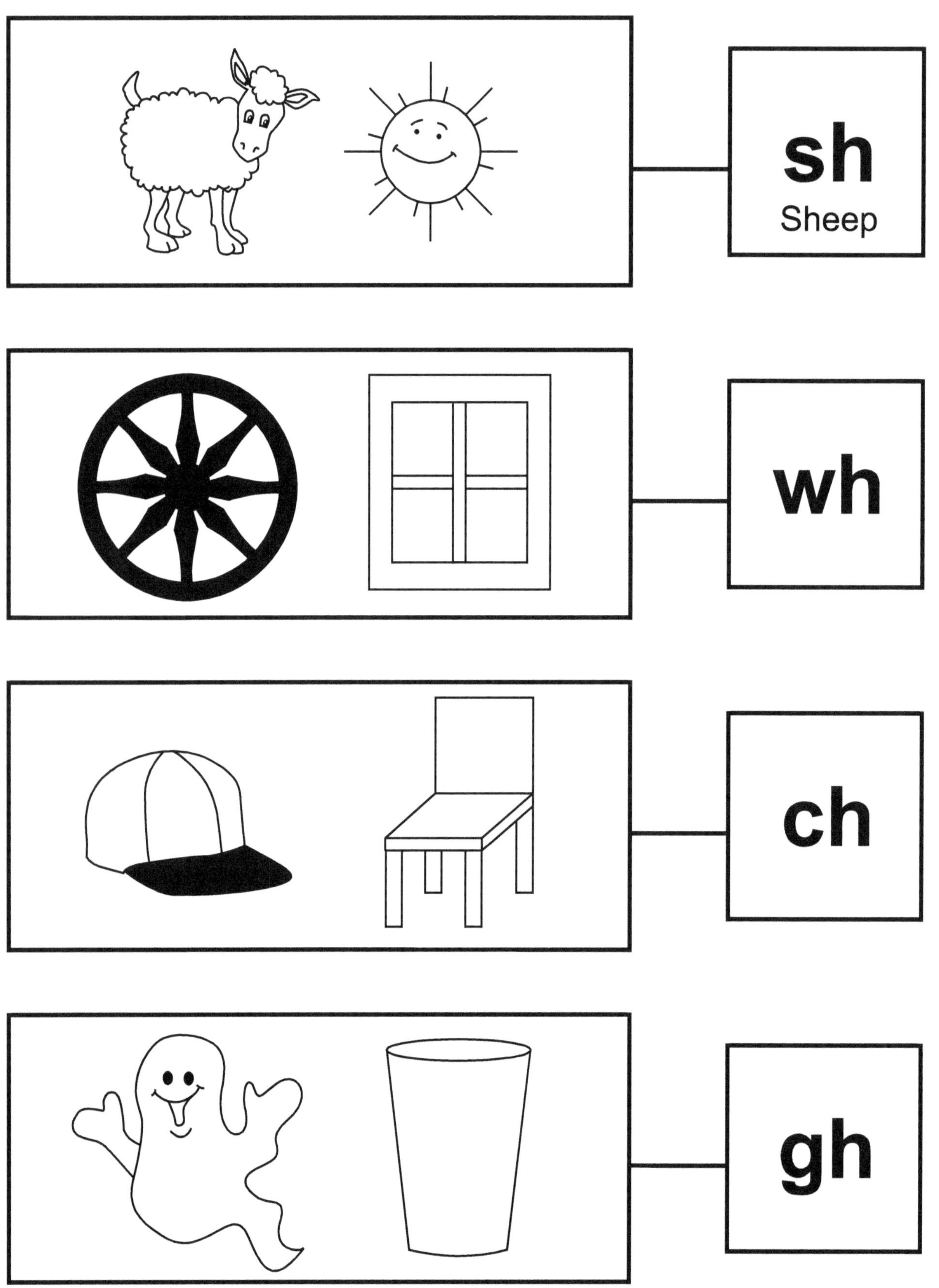

Jumbo English Activity-1

Look at the pictures shown below and finish the sentences by filling in the missing letters.

1. The dog is lapping mi ____ .

2. Butterfly is sitting on a ____ er.

3. The house has t____ windows.

4. There is a lo____ in the pond.

Questions are complete but answers are not. Complete the answers by filling the blanks after a careful look at the pictures.

1. What does Monty like to play with?

   Monty likes to play with _____________

2. Where do birds live?

   Birds live on the _____________

3. How many toffees are lying on the table?

   There are _____ toffees lying on
   the table.

4. What does Leena like to wear?

   Leena likes to wear _____________

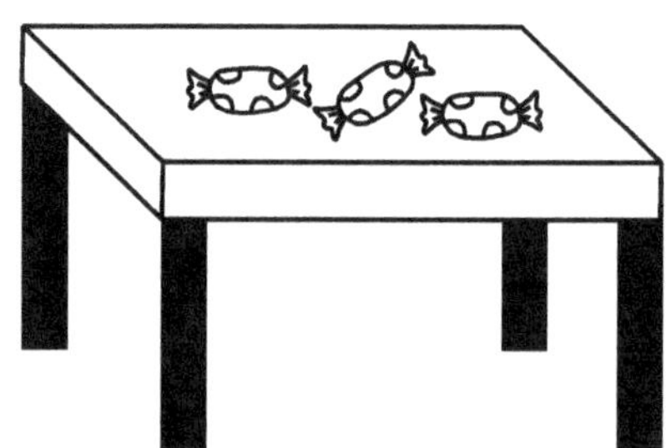

5. What do you like to eat?

   I like to eat _____________

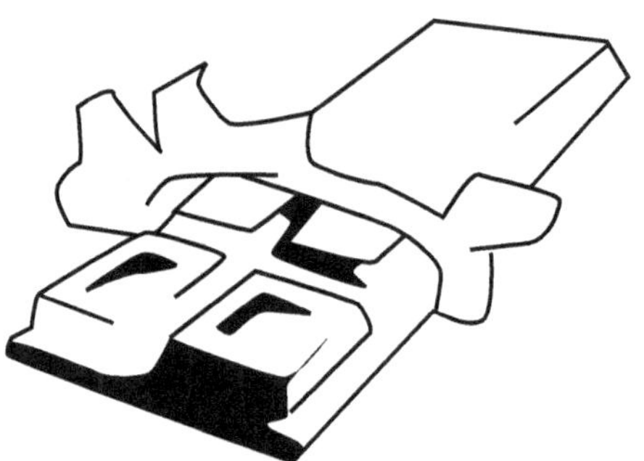

Jumbo English Activity-

See the key words given at the bottom and write correct word for each object.

Two words are given at the end of each sentence. Write correct words in the blanks after looking at the pictures.

There is a .... flying in the sky. (Aeroplane/Kite)

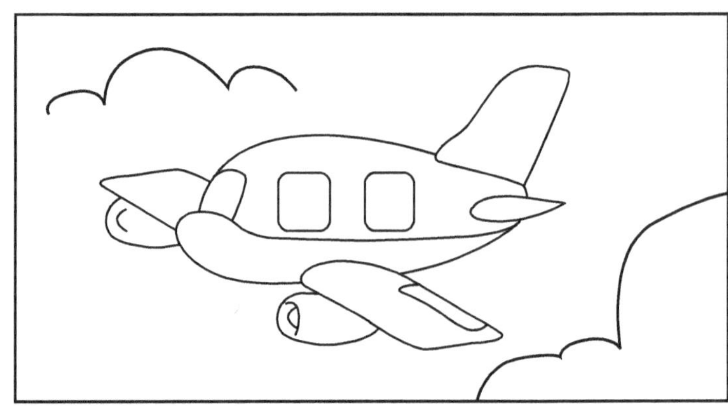

Rohit is feeling .... (Hungry/Sleepy).

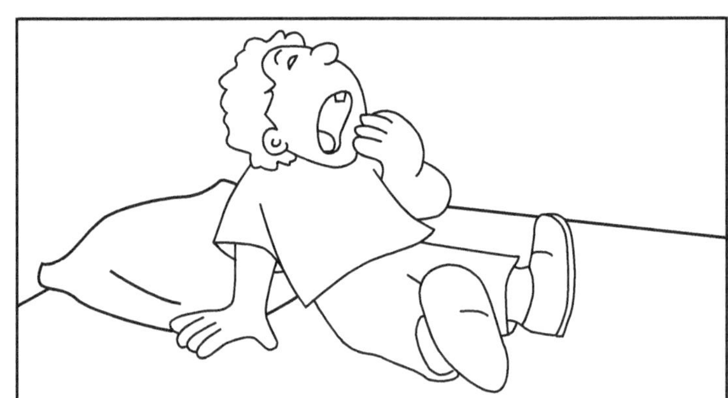

The chef is going to cook .... (Food/Tea).

Santa is skiing on the .... (Snow/Desert).

Look at the faces shown below. Write down the expressions on each chosen from the words given below.

● SCARED   ● HAPPY   ● SAD   ● SURPRISED

Label the picture by putting correct word against each arrow.

Jumbo English Activity–

See the pictures and finish the sentences given below.

Taking help of the key words fill in the blanks to complete the poem.

Little Miss Muffet ______ on a tuffet,
Eating her ______ and ______ .

There came a big ______ ,
Who sat down ______ her.
And ______ Miss Muffet away!

curd   beside   spider
frightened   whey   sat

Jumbo English Activity-1

Fill in the blanks with correct words.

can / cannot

1. A giraffe .... eat leaves from a tall tree.

2. Ducks .... fly in the sky.

3. Animals .... talk.

4. Camel .... run on the sand.

Complete the crossword. Look at the pictures for clues.

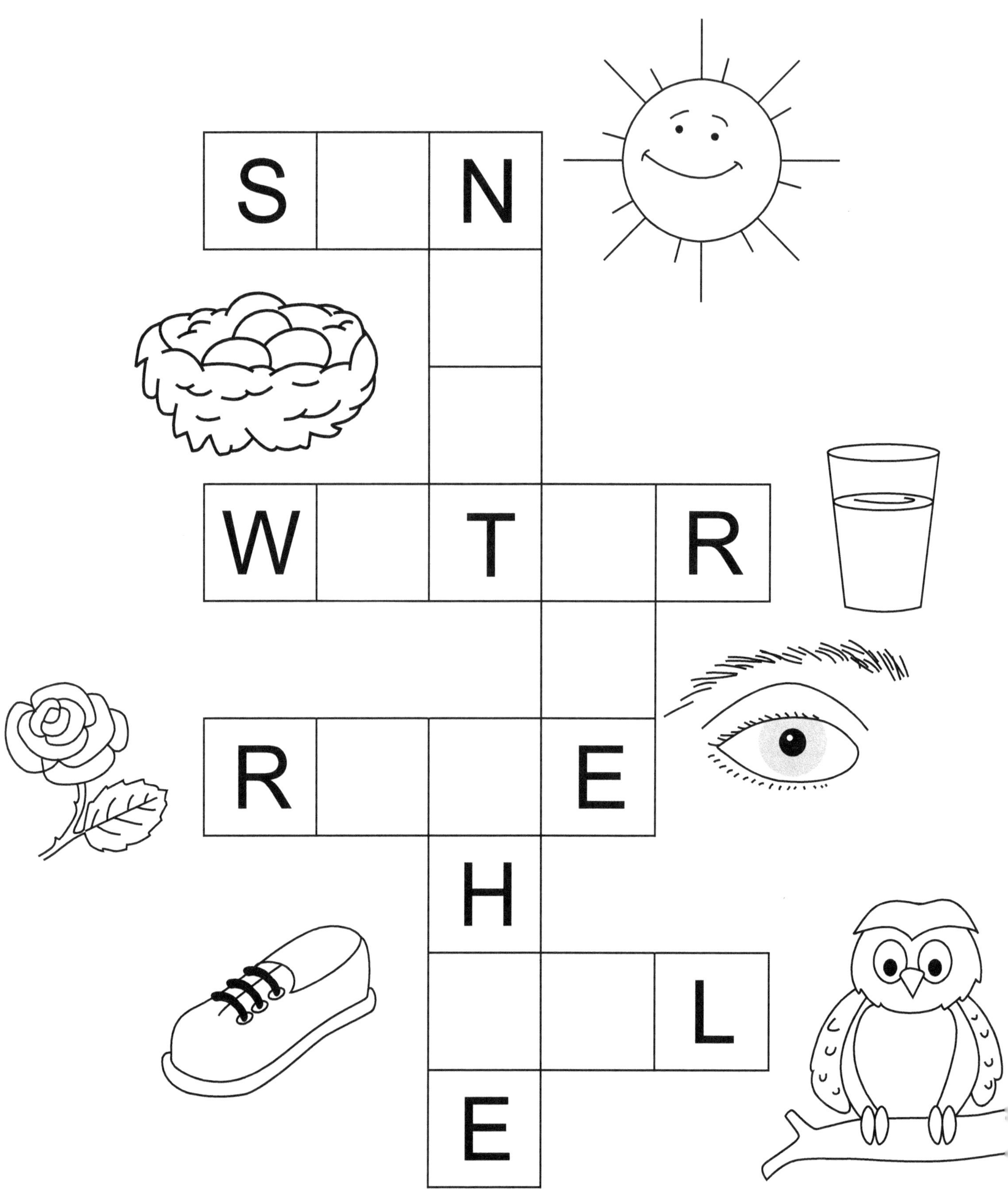

Jumbo English Activity–

See the objects and the sentences. Put the correct serial number of the sentence in the box under each picture.

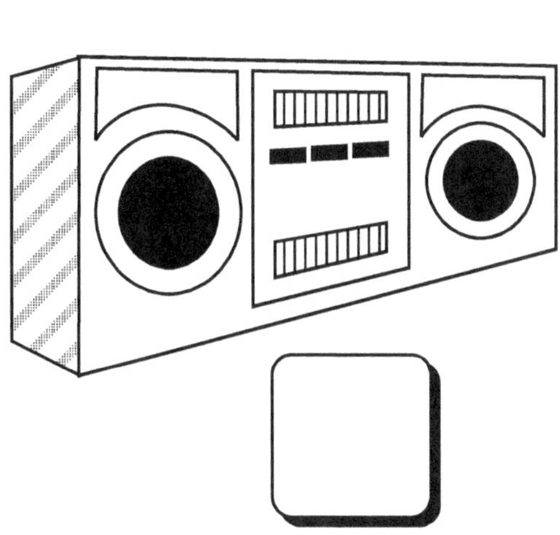 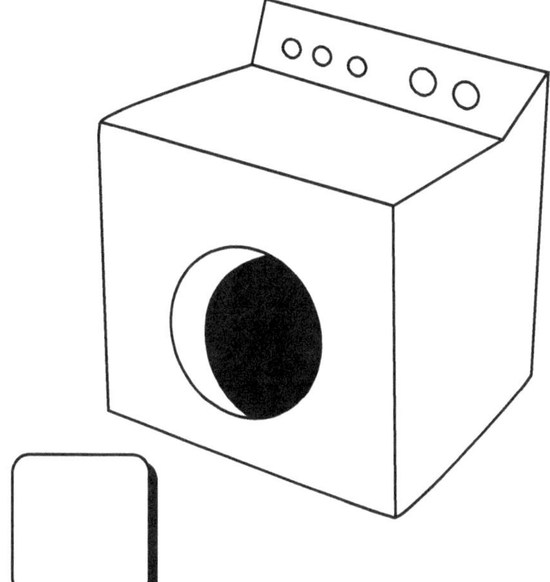

1. We use it to wash clothes.
2. We use it to cook food.
3. We use it to iron clothes.
4. We use it to listen to the music.
5. We use it to keep things cool.

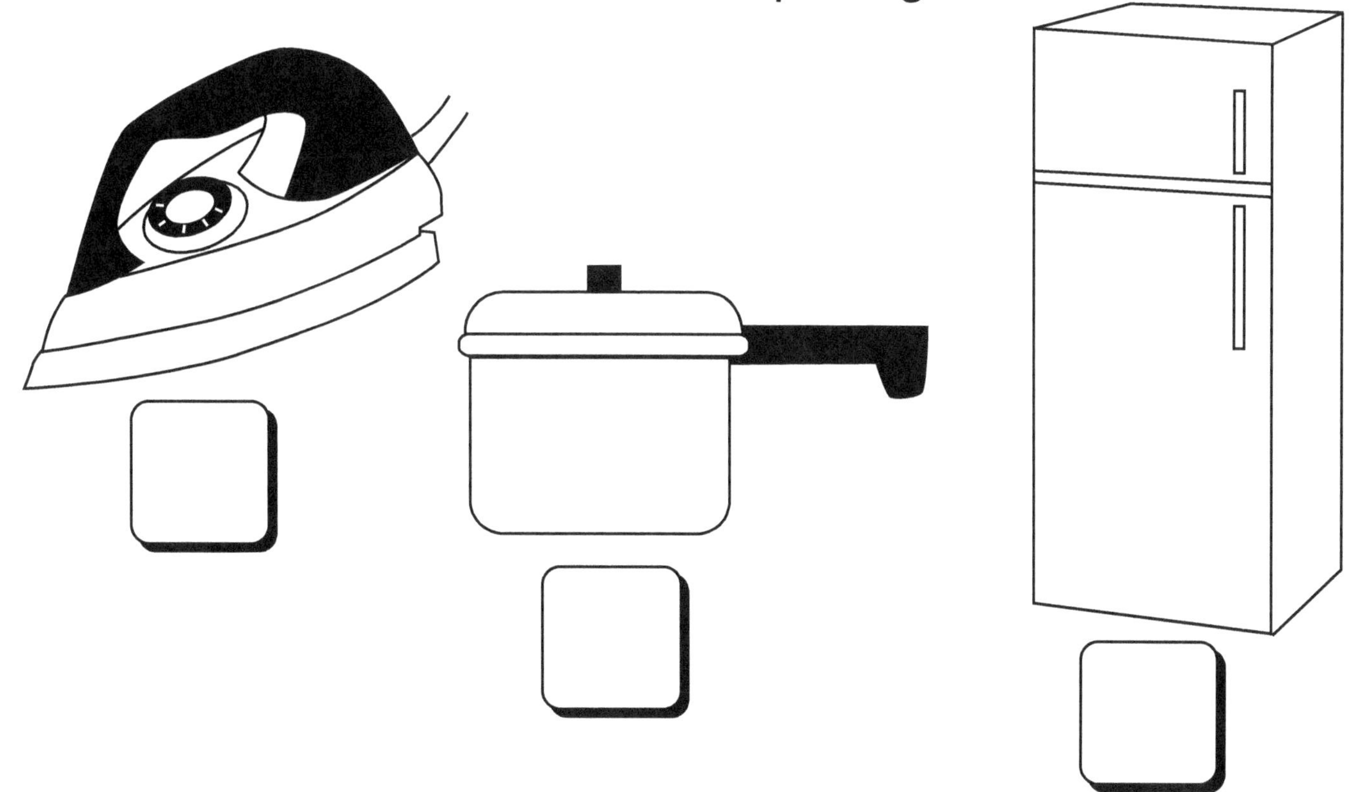

Here are four professionals for you to recognise. It is a who is who like puzzle for you.

MR. GEORGE

1. Mr. Ghanshyam is a ....

2. Mr. Ramesh is a ....

3. Miss Sushmita is a ....

4. Mr. Sunder is a ....

MR. ARTHUR

MR. HARRY

MISS OLIVIA

Jumbo English Activity-1

Read the words given below. Add 's' or 'es' to get their plurals.

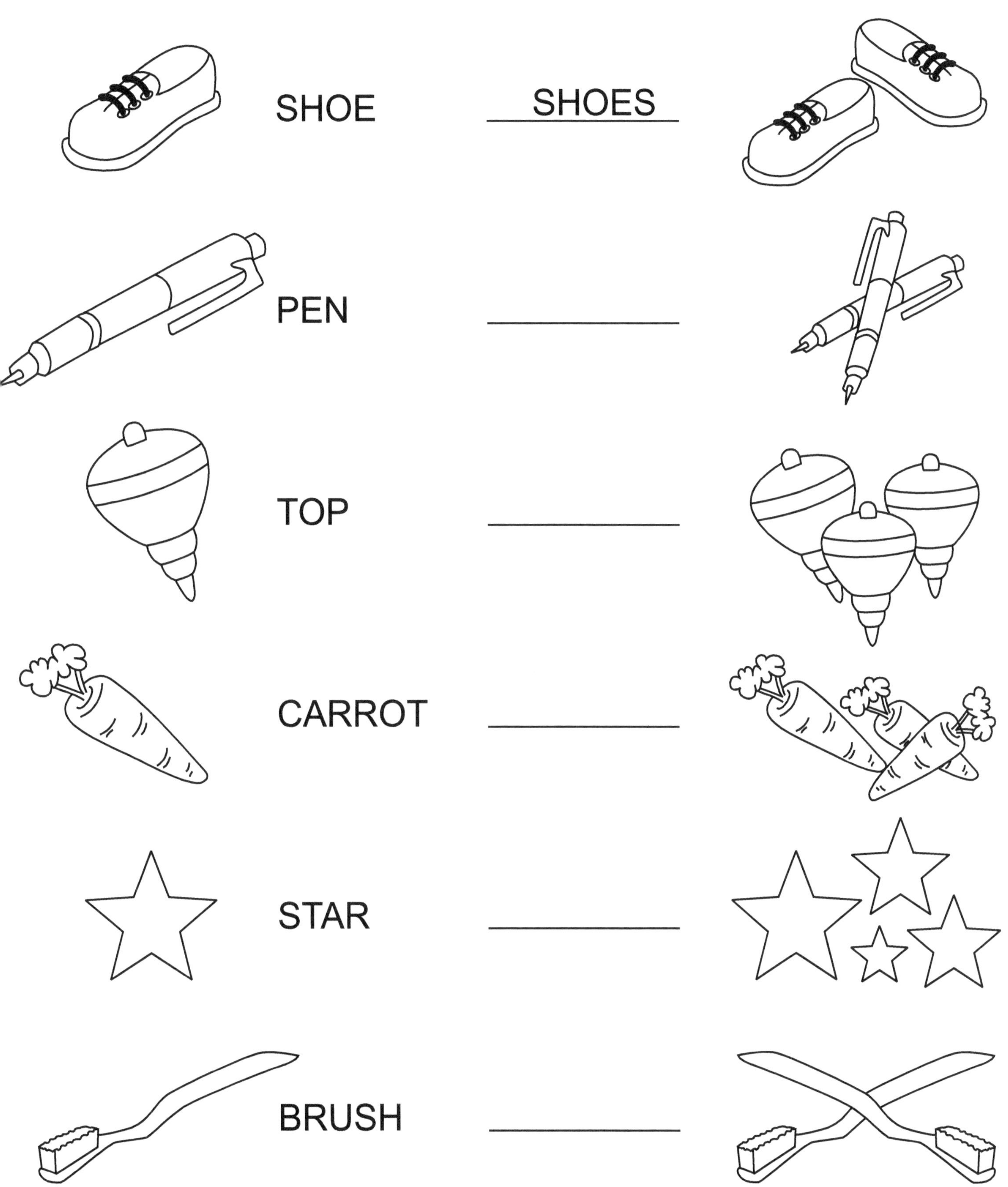

Put the words in a correct order to make the sentences meaningful.
An example.

goes Rohan school to

Rohan goes to school
....

runs fast Rabbit very

....

to picnic go will We

....

deep Sea is very

....

the in Sun sky shines

....

clever Owl bird is a

....

Jumbo English Activity–

Colour the pictures after carefully reading the sentences.

1. Sun is Yellow.

2. It is a beautiful Pink frock.

3. Rinku will wear Blue shoes
    for the party.

4. We saw an Orange fish
    in the pond.

5. Leaves of plants are Green.

Every word has three forms. After examining the sample word write other two forms of the each word.

HOT	HOTTER	HOTTEST
THIN	....	....
....	TALLER	....
....	....	BIGGEST
BRIGHT	....	....
....	HARDER	....
....	....	SHORTEST
FAT	....	....

Jumbo English Activity-1

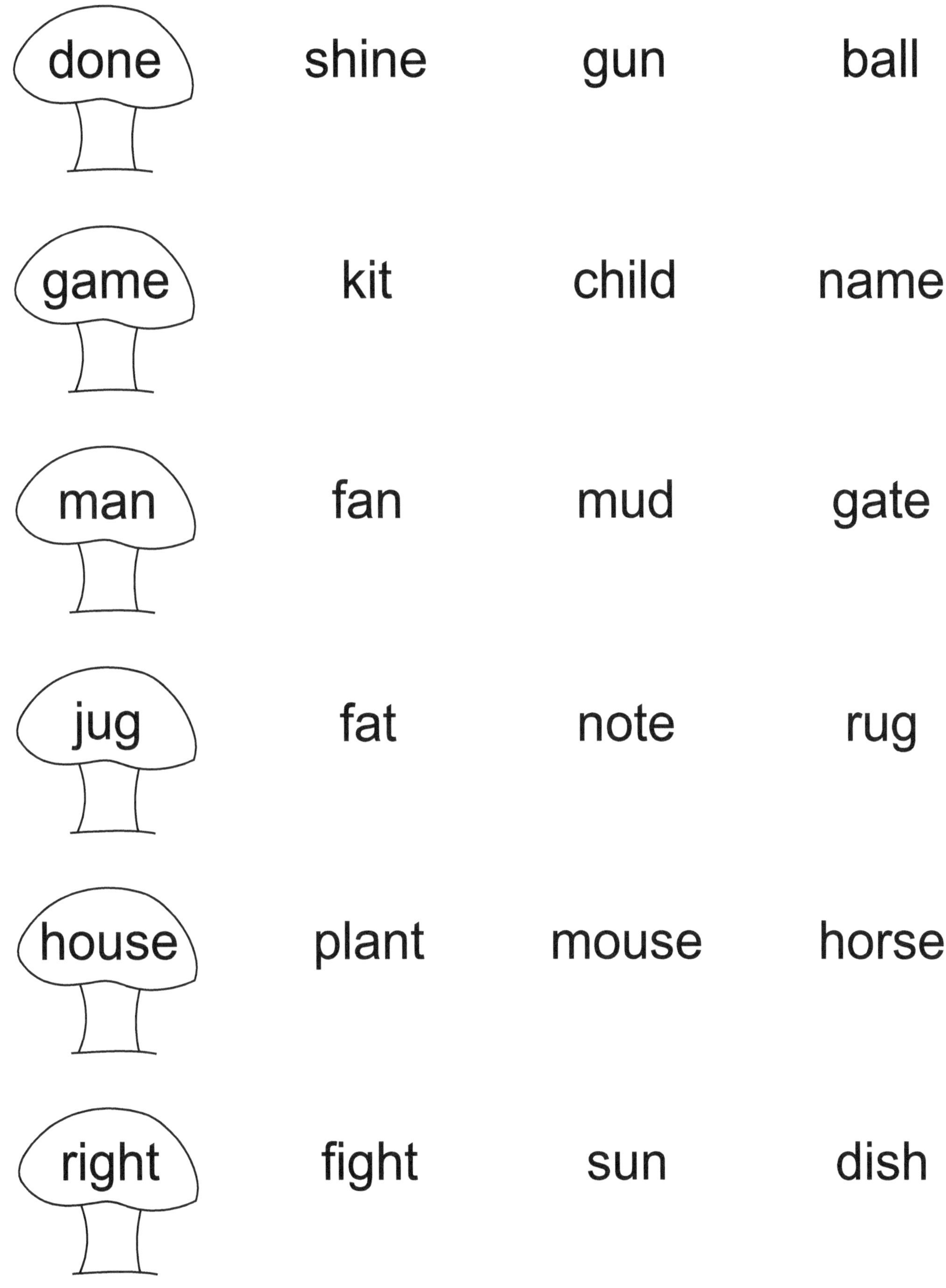

done   shine   gun   ball
game   kit   child   name
man   fan   mud   gate
jug   fat   note   rug
house   plant   mouse   horse
right   fight   sun   dish

Colour the biggest and the smallest object in each group.

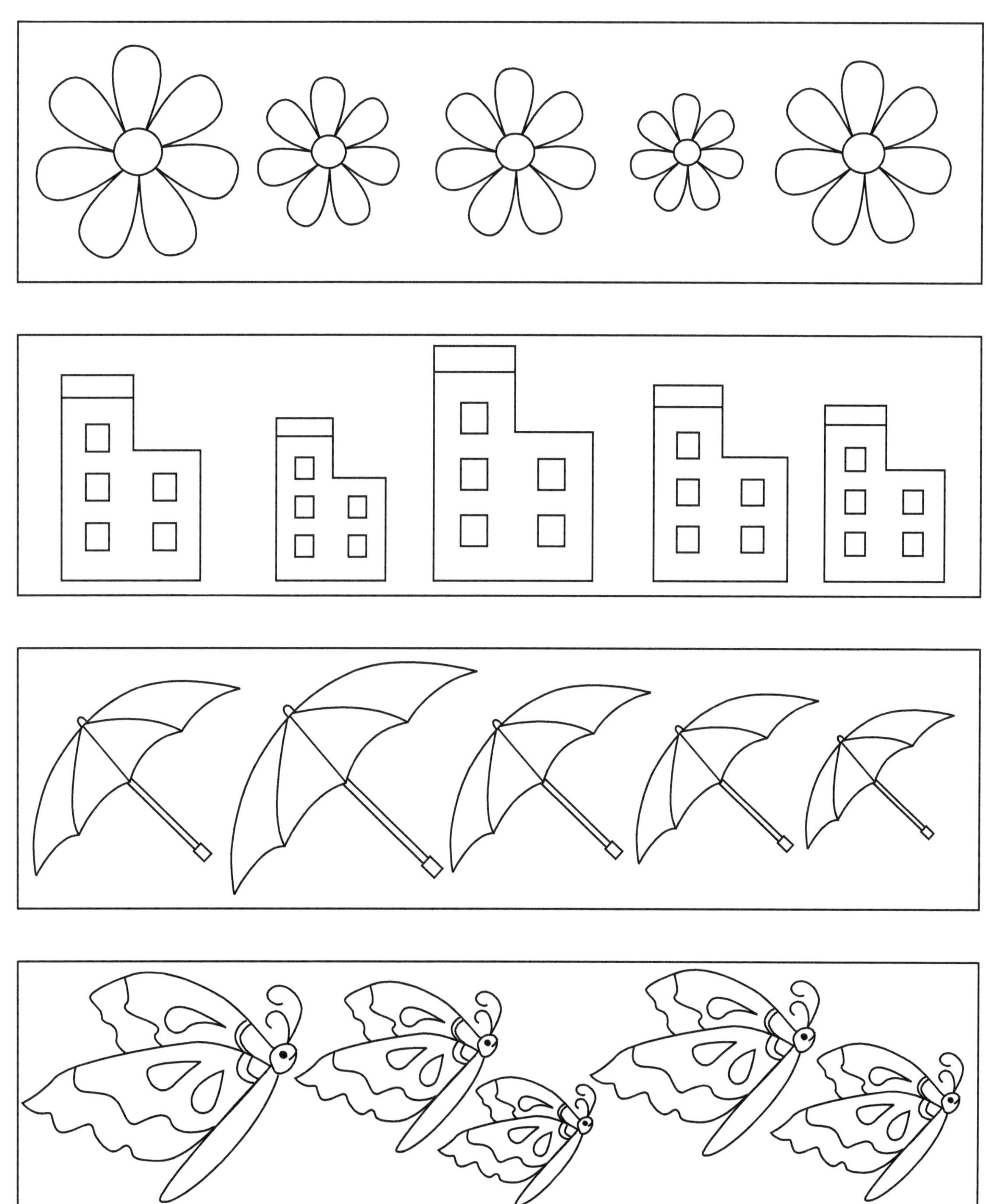

Colour the object whose name ends with the letter written at your left.

Match the words in small letters to the ones in capital letters.

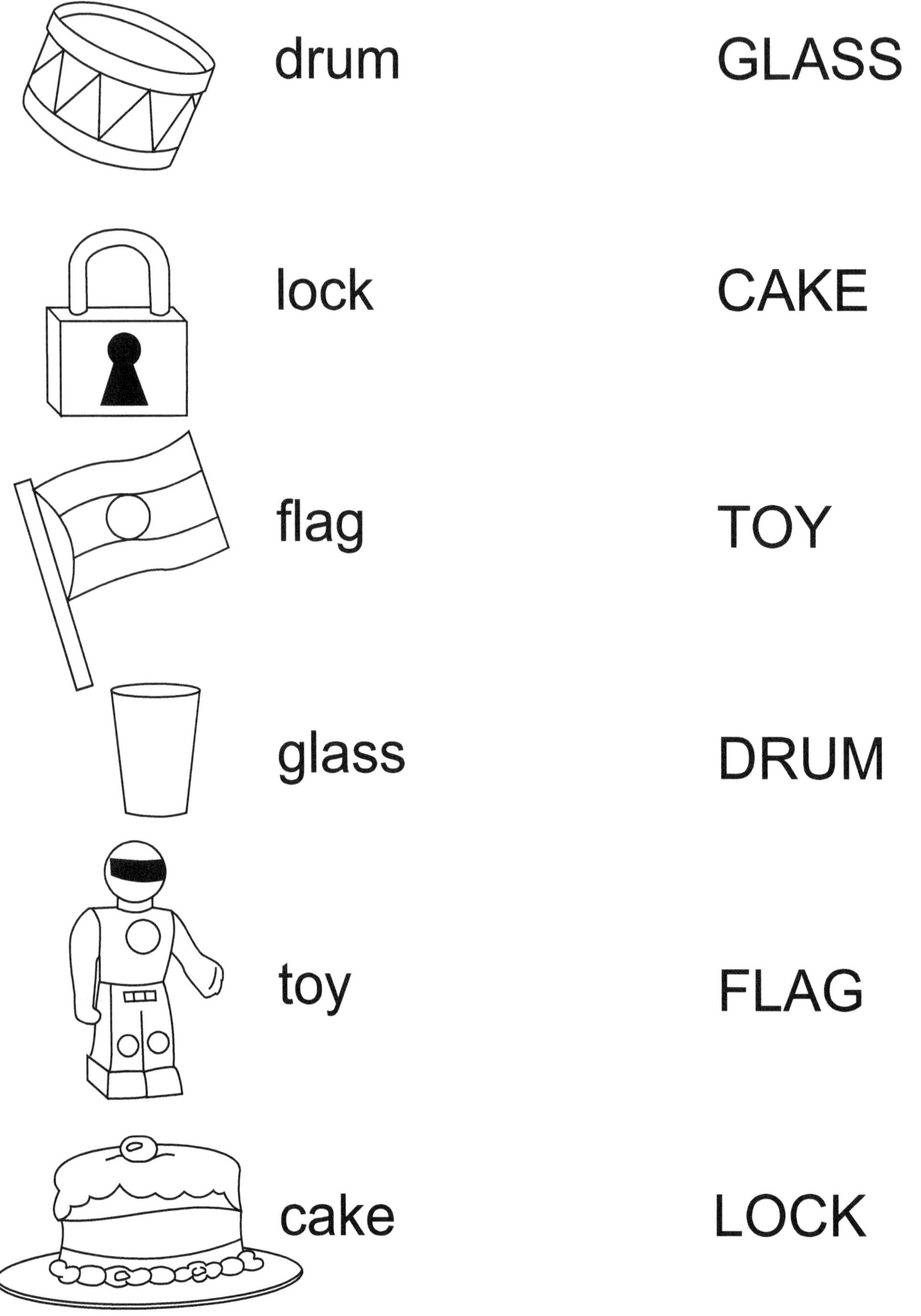

Jumbo English Activity–1

Identify the objects, complete the words and colour the pictures.

J....G

....OO....

C....OC....

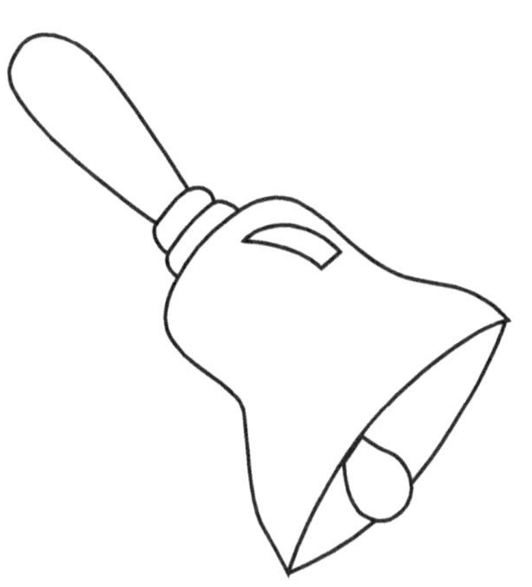

BE.... ....

....ISH

CL....W....

Left side numbers have rhyming objects pictured at right. Pair them with a straight line as shown in Two and Shoe.

Jumbo English Activity–

Fill in the blanks with opposites of the words after seeing the picture carefully.

1. Tony is fat.

    Golu is ....

2. Horse has............. tail

    Pig has short tail.

3. Elephant is big.

    Bird is ....

4. Water is ....

    Coffee is hot.

Tick the correct one of the words given under each picture.

BE / BEE

TYRE / TIRE

SUN / SON

ICE / EYES

Jumbo English Activity-1

Write the missing vowels to get the names of the objects pictured at left.

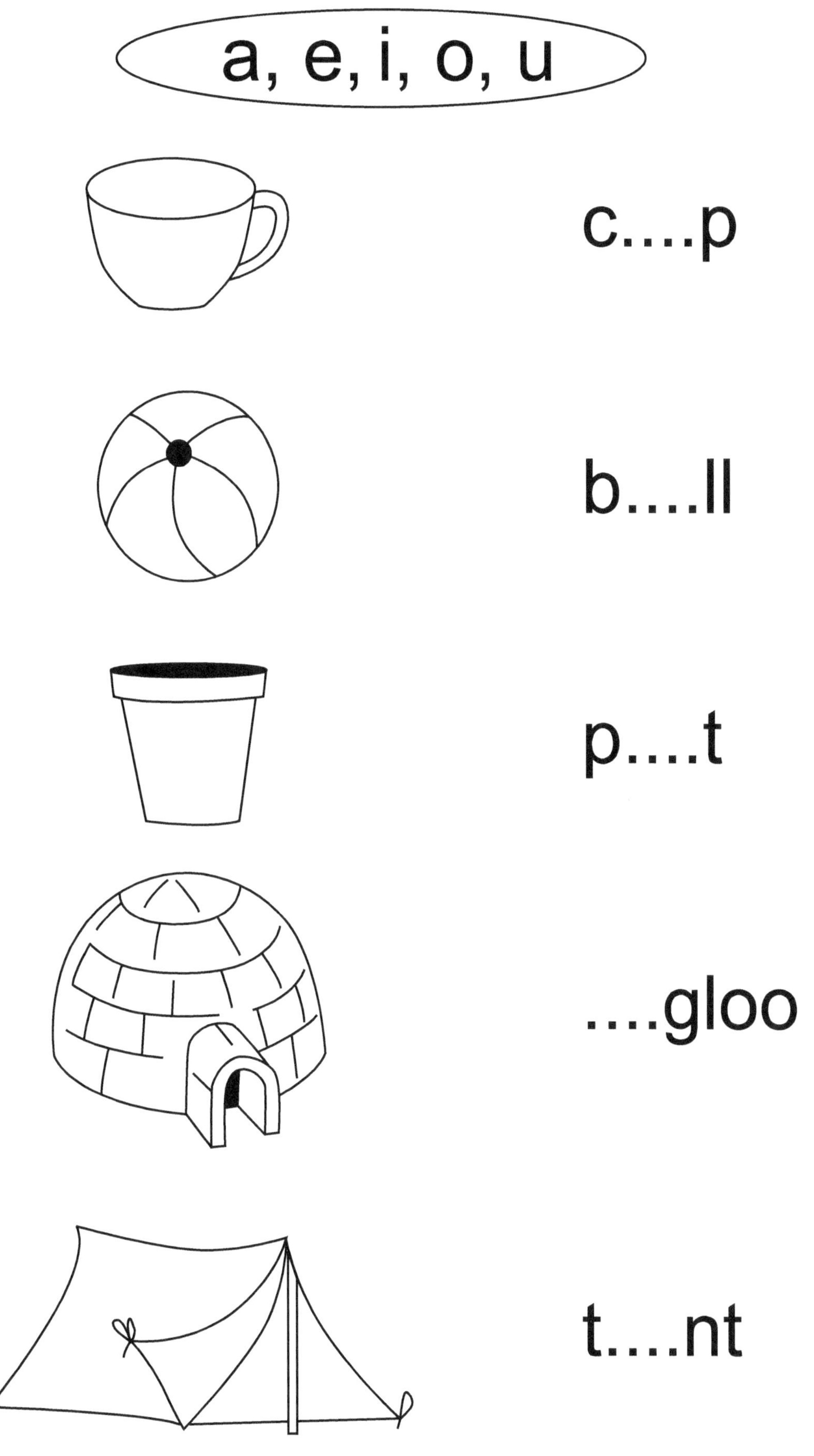

a, e, i, o, u

c....p

b....ll

p....t

....gloo

t....nt

See the pictures and write action word for each character.

sweeping, sleeping, reading, playing, eating

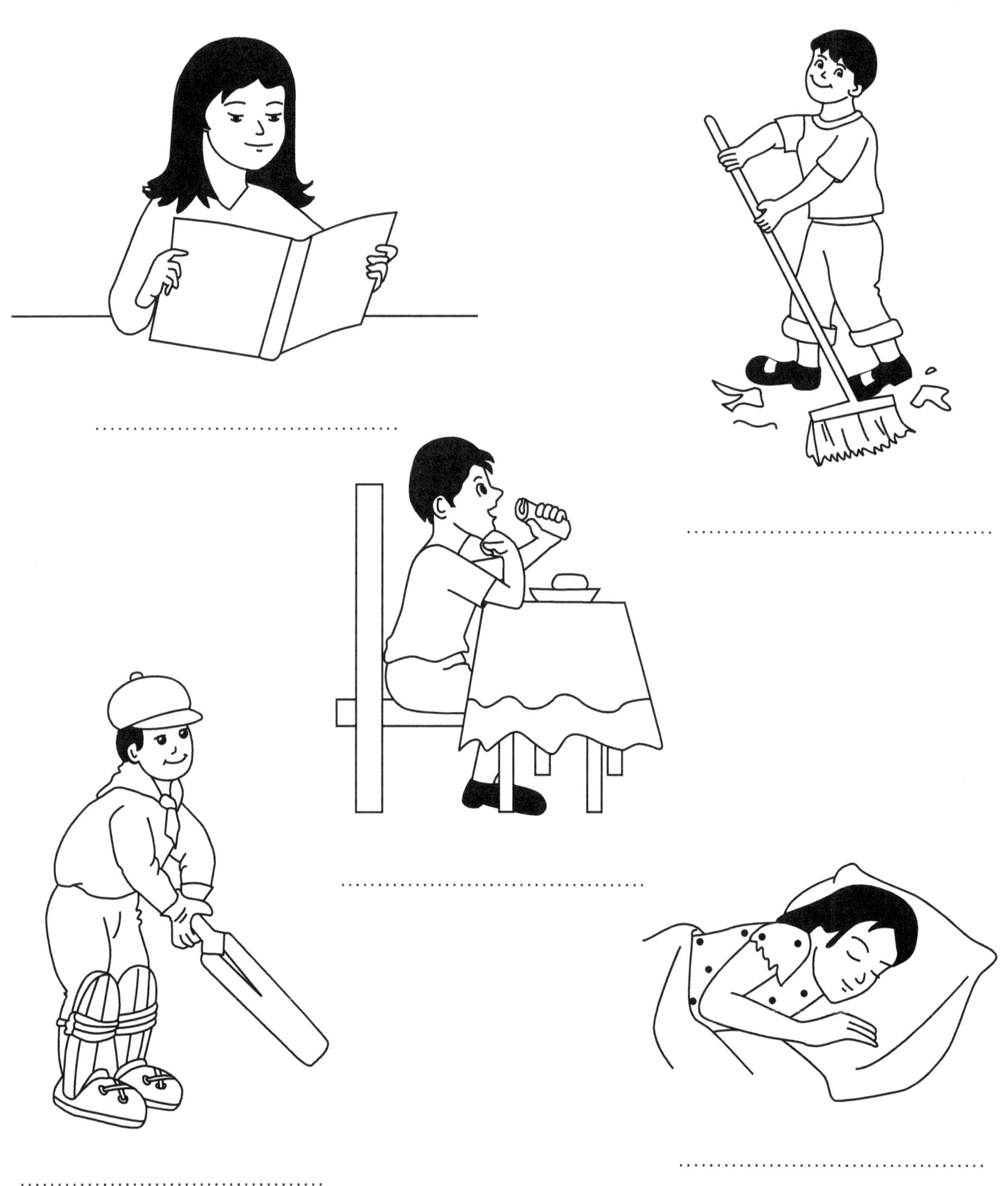

Jumbo English Activity–

Unscramble the words and write them in the blanks.

1. The dog likes to eat ....(eobn)

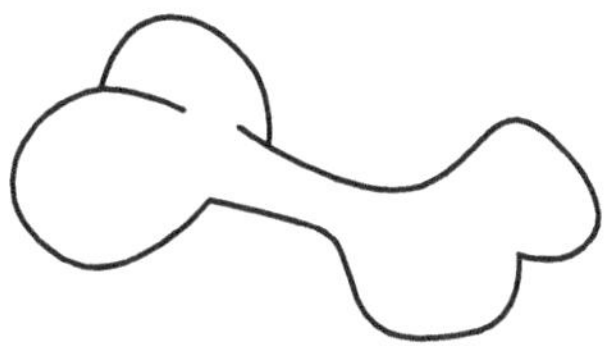

2. This is my .... (chosol)

3. A .... (dirb) is sitting on the tree.

4. Clouds are in the ....(kys)

5. These are my school .... (sehos).

Neeru's friends have hidden her bag. Decode the message to see where they have hid it. Use the code keys given at the bottom.

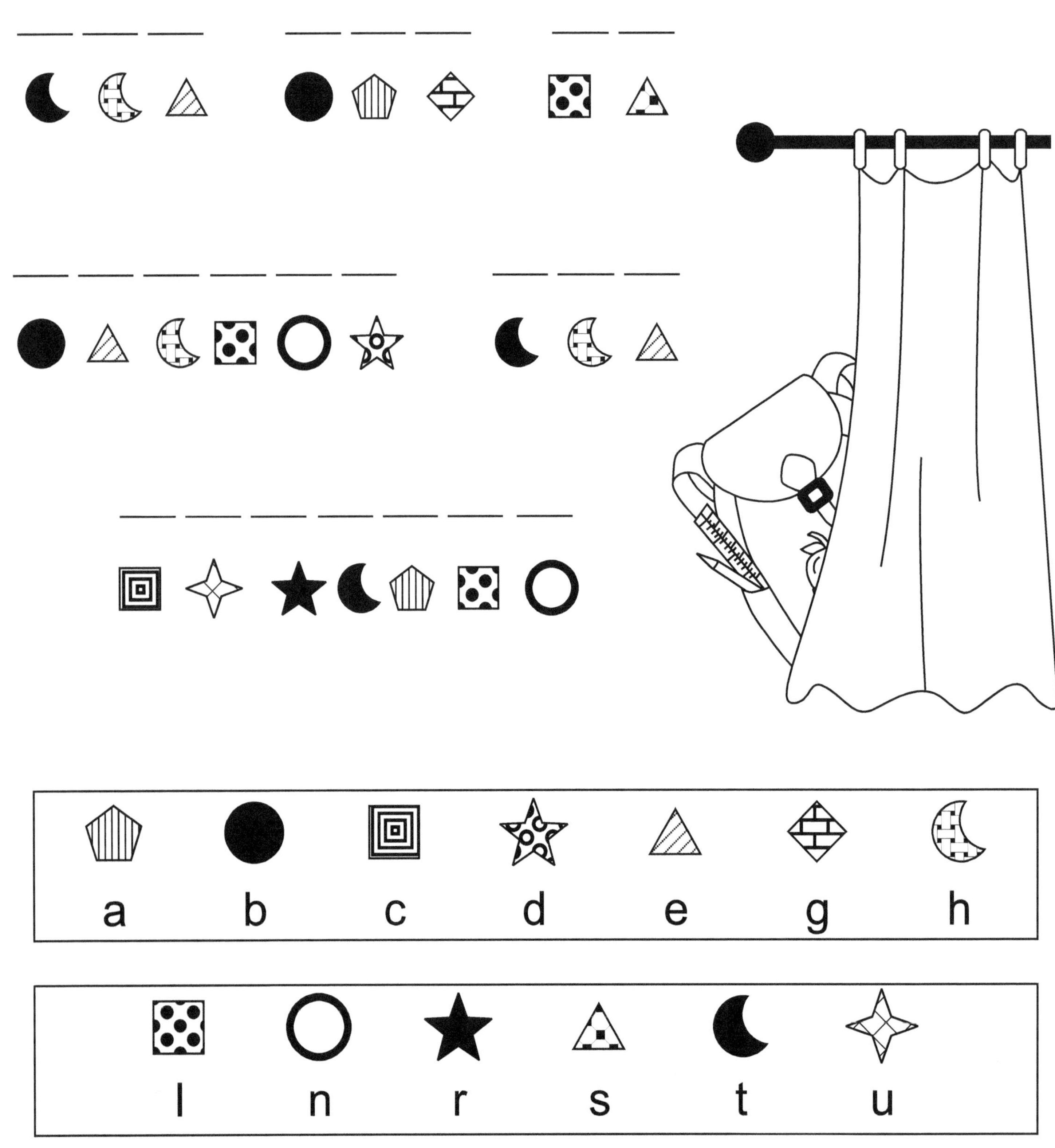

Look at the pictures shown below. You have to identify the bigger ones in each group and colour them.

Draw a line to join the animals to their calls.

Jumbo English Activity–

Fill in the blanks with has/have.

> Has is used for one person.
> Have is used for many persons.
> Have is also used for I
> e.g. I <u>have</u> a brown dog.

1. She .... two toffees.

2. I .... many colourful pencils.

3. Monu .... three balloons.

4. I .... to go to school early today.

5. Tina .... two pet dogs.

6. He .... a blue watch.

7. They .... a big house.

8. Ram and Shyam .... a chocolate each.

Write the correct answers in the blanks.

1. This is a .... (spoon / fork)

2. Nita is .... (sleeping / reading)

3. There are .... (two / three)
    flowers in the pot.

4. My pillow has .... (dots / lines)
    printed on it.

5. Bird is .... (walking / flying)
    in the sky.

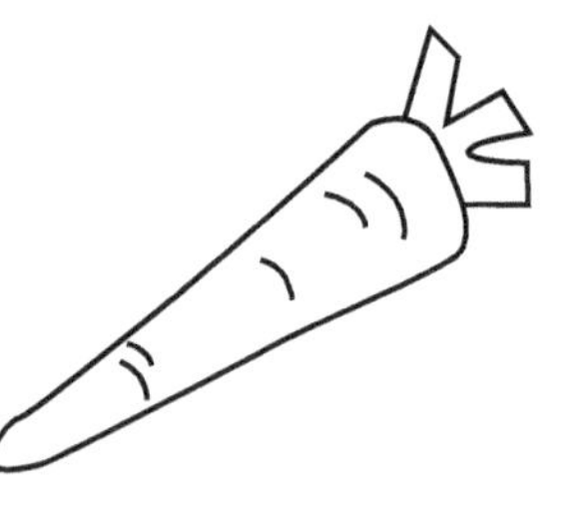

6. Rabbit likes to eat .... (carrot / fish).

Jumbo English Activity-1

Complete the following sentences with the right word from the words given under each sentence.

1. **December** is to **winter** as **June** is to ....

   warmer   month   summer   autumn

   Cake is to **eat** as **milk** is to ....

   drink   cream   holiday   tea

   Christmas is **to merry** as **New Year** is to ....

   celebrate   January   happy   party

   Out is to **in** as **give** is to ....

   gifts   present   help   take

   To is to **two** as **Claus** is to ....

   Santa   Nickle   bend   claws

   A **bus** is to **road** as an **aeroplane** is to ....

   water   sky   play   big

Dinky loves gardening. She has bought two plants.
One has red flowers and other has yellow flowers. She has
planted them in small pots and kept them in her garden.

1. What is the girl's name?

....

2. What does she like to do?

....

3. What are the colours of her flowers?

....

4. Where did she plant the flowers?

....

Jumbo English Activity–

Given below are few sentences. If you think a particular sentence is complete write 'Y', if not, write 'N'in the box. An example is given below.

I found on the table. **N**

I found a pencil on the table. **Y**

1. Food on the plate. ☐

2. I like to eat chocolates. ☐

3. What you doing here? ☐

4. Jack put the keys in his coat. ☐

5. Don't dance the rain. ☐

6. Go market buy fruits. ☐

Look at the pictures. Colour the faster animal of each pair.

Jumbo English Activity-1

In each group cross out the odd word.

bake   shake   make   take

January   Saturday   April   September

tie   shirt   mango   shoes

circle   square   two   oval

hen   deer   elephant   lion

ball   wicket   car   bat

In jumbled words hiden the names of animals. Find them and write in the boxes.

maelc

erde

nloi

woc

tlepaneh

eorsh

odg

tac

rofg

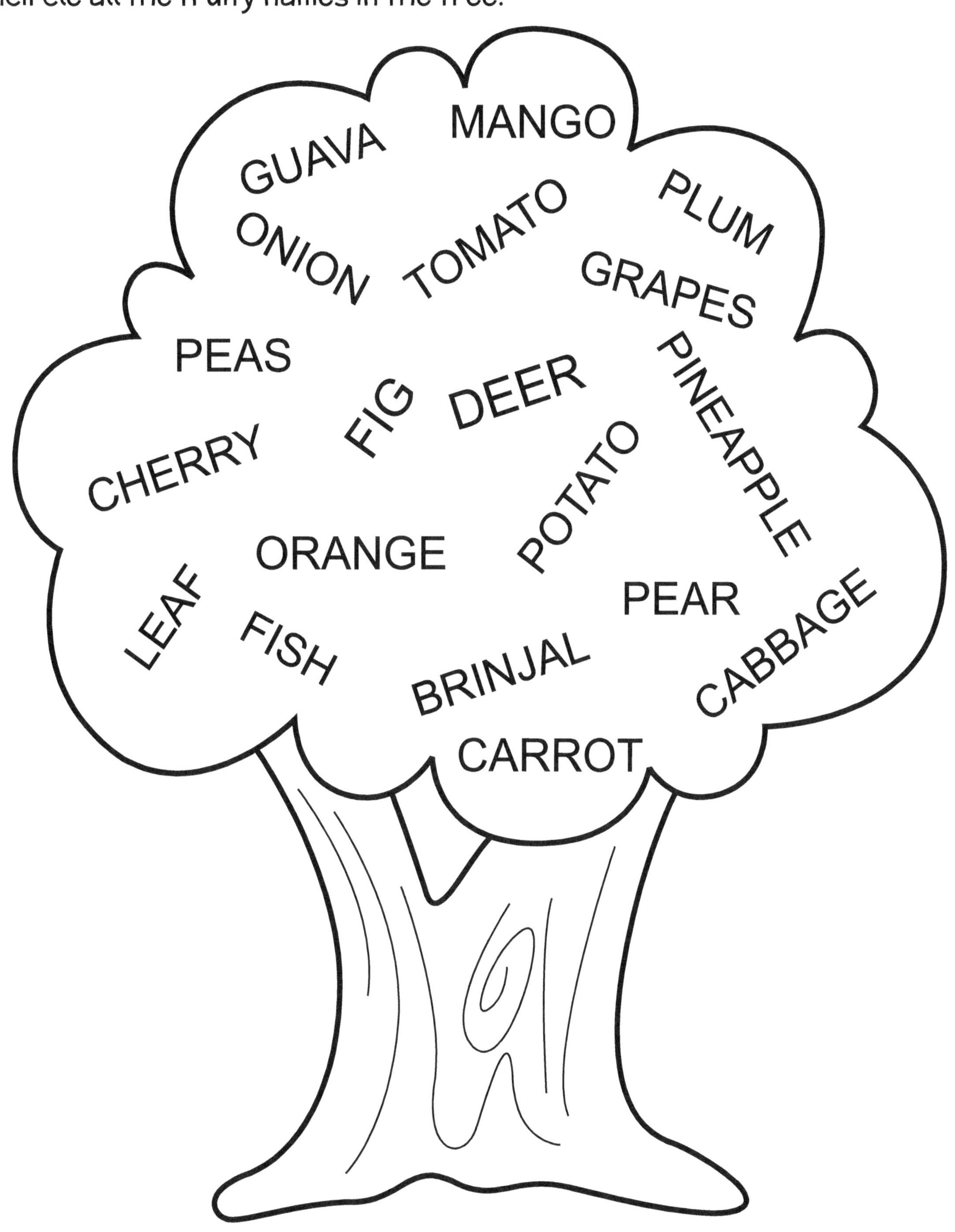

GUAVA
MANGO
PLUM
ONION
TOMATO
GRAPES
PEAS
FIG
DEER
PINEAPPLE
CHERRY
POTATO
ORANGE
PEAR
LEAF
FISH
BRINJAL
CABBAGE
CARROT

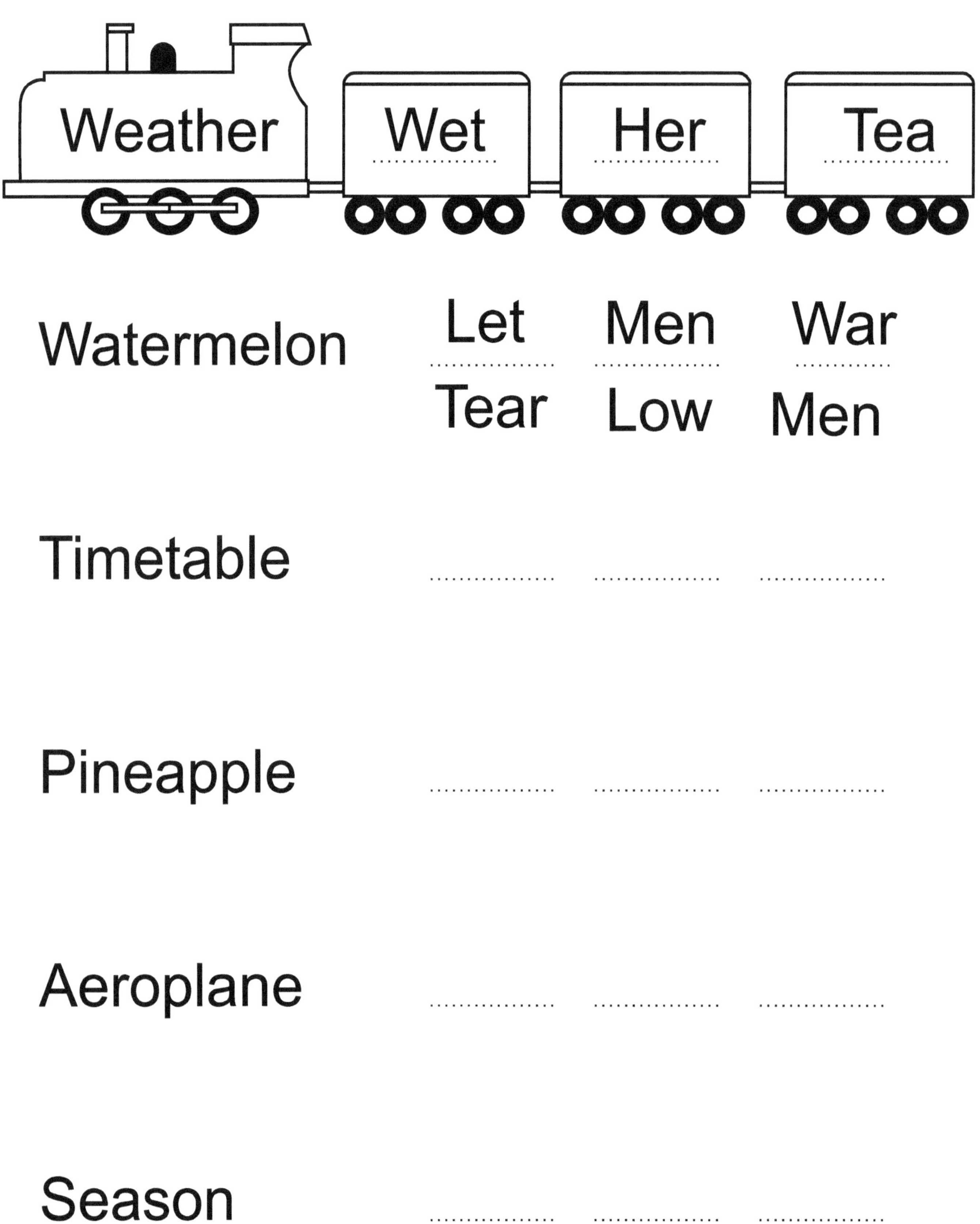

Watermelon	Let	Men	War
	Tear	Low	Men
Timetable			
Pineapple			
Aeroplane			
Season			

It's Siddarth's birthday. He has planned many things for his birthday. Can you find them in the grid given below? Colour them to separate.

B	A	L	L	O	O	N	C	T	C
C	F	T	U	M	R	N	R	Q	A
K	T	O	F	F	E	E	S	Z	K
B	I	L	X	J	V	N	R	G	E
Q	P	T	U	Y	R	O	G	A	E
W	C	A	N	D	L	E	S	M	Y
G	A	K	L	D	R	S	R	E	D
L	R	E	N	A	C	P	H	S	U
P	D	M	G	I	F	T	S	X	Z
Z	S	W	U	X	I	T	N	S	B

BALLOON
CANDLES
CAKE
CARDS
GAMES
GIFTS
TOFFEES

Fill in the correct words from the words given in the brackets.

1. Who .... the race yesterday? (win, won, winner)

2. Nita .... two dolls. (has, have, having)

3. What are you .... ?(ate, eat, eating)

4. Tigers live .... the jungle. (under, in, on)

5. Which baby is the .... of the two? (fat, fatter, fattest)

6. Radhika .... very well. (dances, dance, dancing)

7. My school is .... to my house. (under, near, next)

8. Did you .... to market today? (went, going, go)

Rearrange the given words to get a new word.

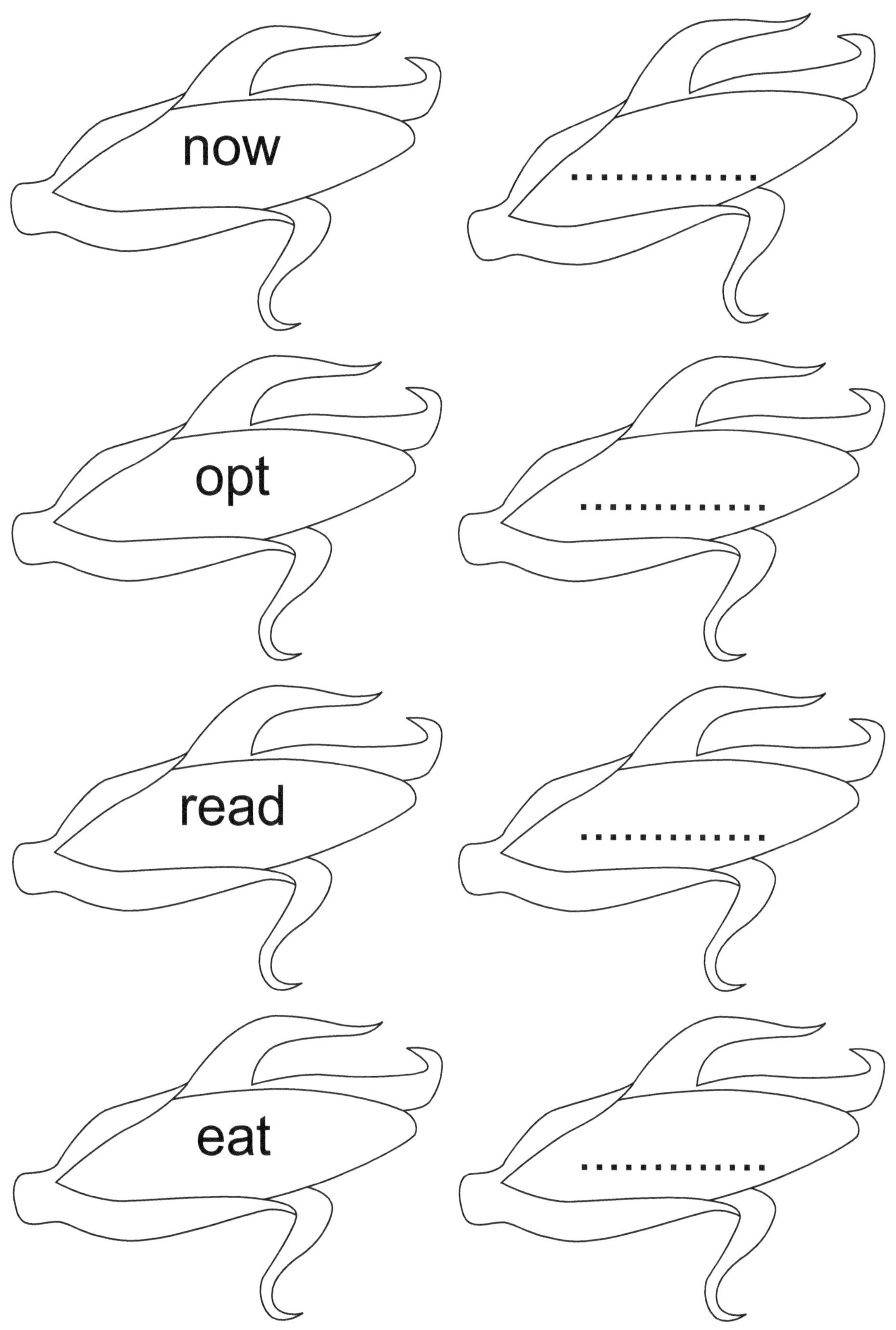

There are two bags for different items. Put the given things in correct bag.

FROCK

TOMATO

BANANA

CAP

TIE

BELT

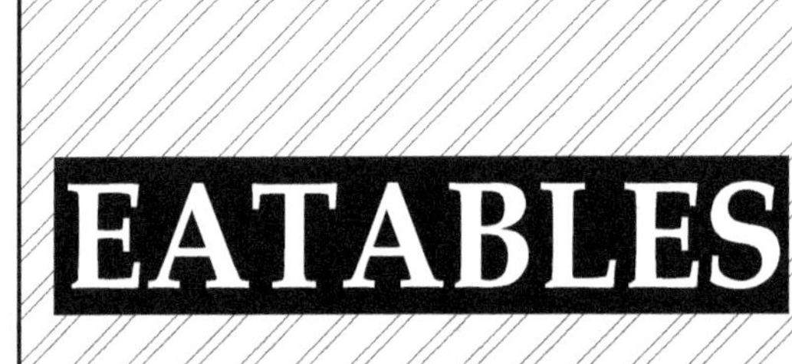

SOCKS

PASTRY

BREAD

RICE

MANGO

BOW

Jumbo English Activity-1

Gaurav likes to eat and Saurav likes to play. Fill their almirahs with things of their choice.

Find the body parts written below in the crossword grid. Colour them to separate.

P	E	Y	E	A	C	F	O	G	R
M	S	T	V	K	B	L	I	P	S
A	C	H	I	N	S	U	M	T	N
F	J	E	S	O	Q	Z	A	K	E
H	A	N	D	S	W	N	I	D	C
E	J	K	A	E	P	T	S	C	K
D	G	O	I	R	E	A	R	S	U
A	R	M	F	X	A	I	M	D	K
B	Y	H	E	J	L	F	E	E	T
S	T	O	M	A	C	H	Z	C	G

FEET   EARS

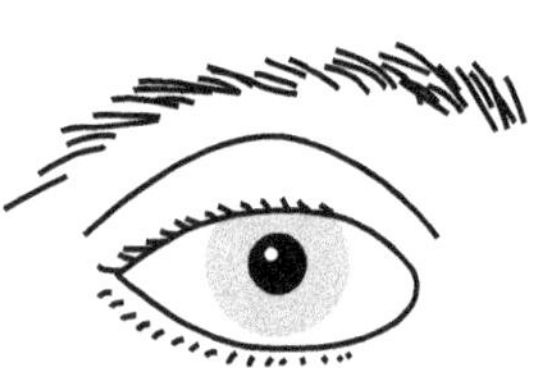

EYE   ARM

LIPS   NECK

HANDS   STOMACH

NOSE   CHIN

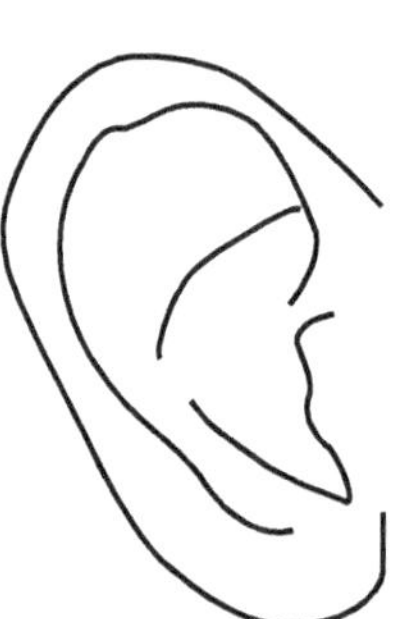

Jumbo English Activity-

Colour the correct picture in the group. Two initial letters give the clues.

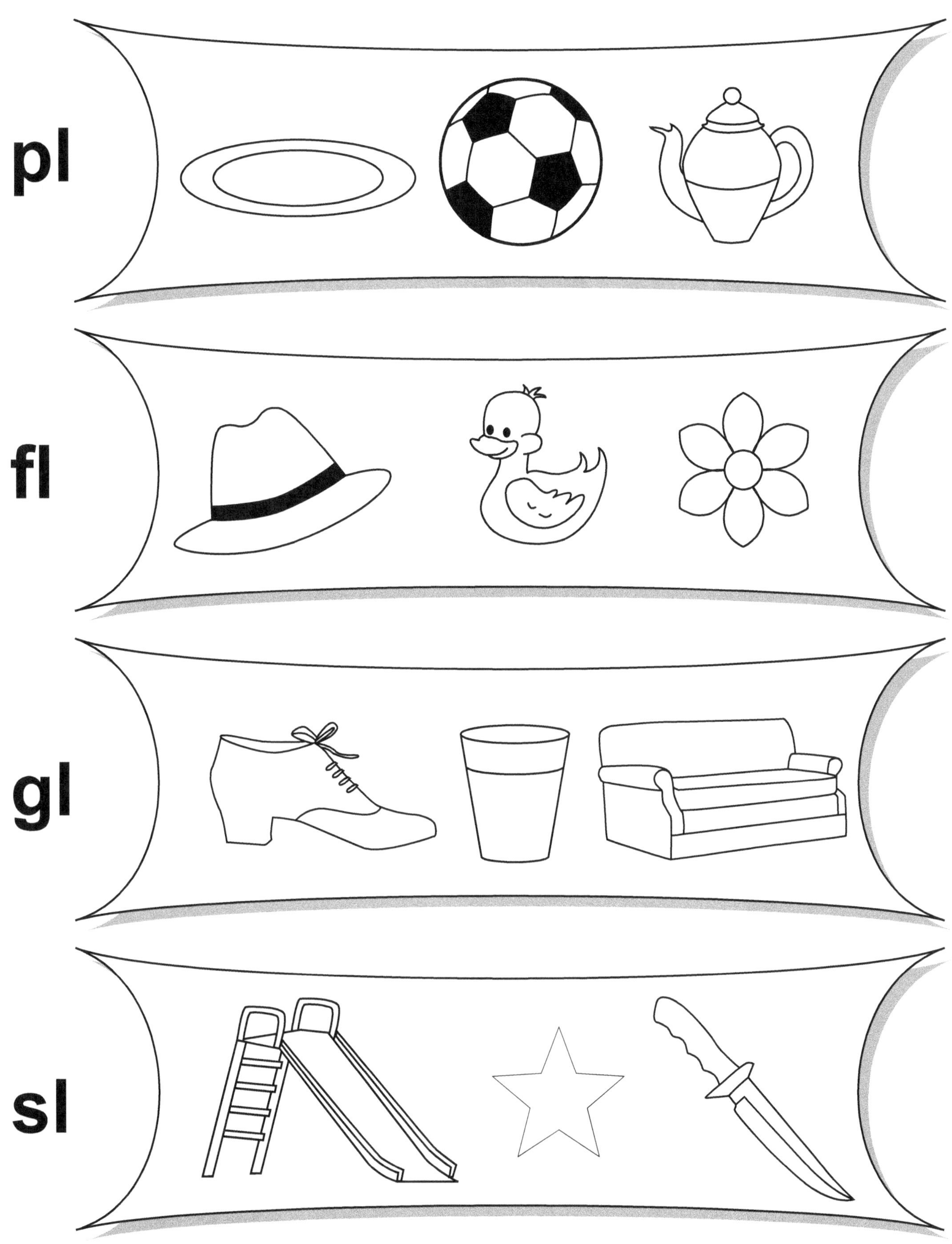

pl

fl

gl

sl

Identify the pictures and tick the correct options.

 **BURGER / PASTRY**

 **WATCH / CLOCK**

 **TREE / FLOWER**

 **DOOR / BELL**

 **SHOES / SOCKS**

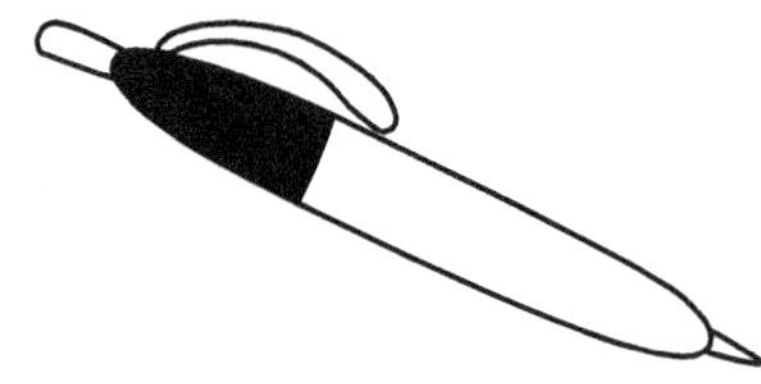 **PEN / PENCIL**

Jumbo English Activity-1

Distribute the words into the categories which they belong to.

Pear	Rose	Ginger
Daisy	Orange	Tomato
Brinjal	Sunflower	Banana
Mango	Lily	Ladyfinger

FLOWERS

____

____

____

____

FRUITS

____

____

____

____

VEGETABLES

____

____

____

____

One, Two,

Buckle my ....

Three, Four,

Shut the ....

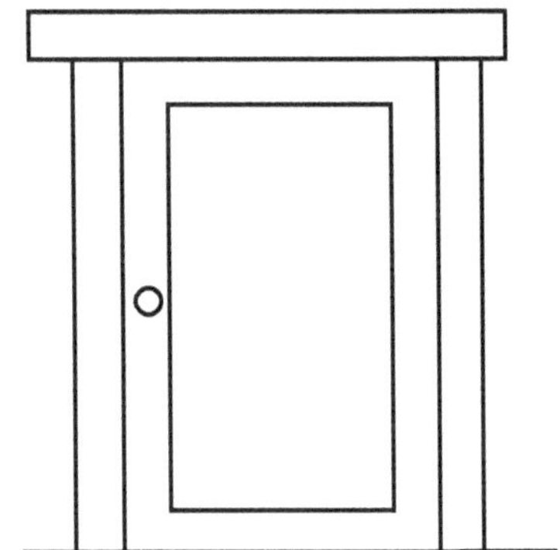

Five, Six,

Pick up the ....

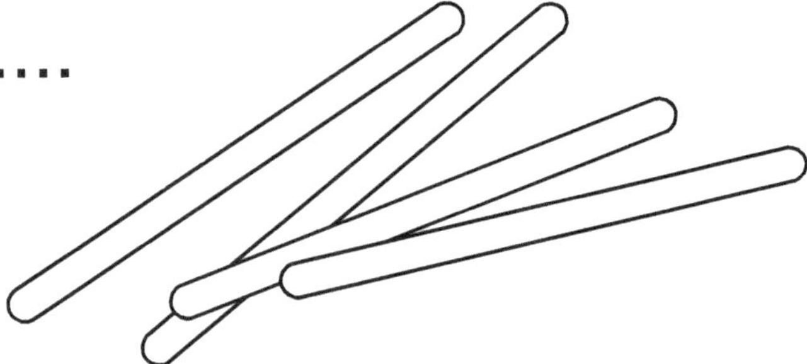

Seven, Eight,

Lay them straight.

Nine, Ten,

A big fat ....

1. Colour of our hair is blue.   ....

2. Birds fly in the sky.   ....

3. Tortoise runs very fast.   ....

4. Animals can talk.   ....

5. Triangle has three corners.   ....

6. Ship sails in the water.   ....

Kaushik has misspelt all the colours. Can you write them correctly for him.

IPNK ....

ONBRW ....

UPPRLE ....

LAKCB ....

REENG ....

WEYOLL ....

EDR ....

BUEL ....

1. Is this a mango?

....

2. Is this a bus?

....

3. Is this a girl?

....

4. Is this a book?

....

5. Is this a toothbrush?

....

6. Is this an aeroplane?

....

Draw wavy lines from the numbers to their word forms as given in the example.

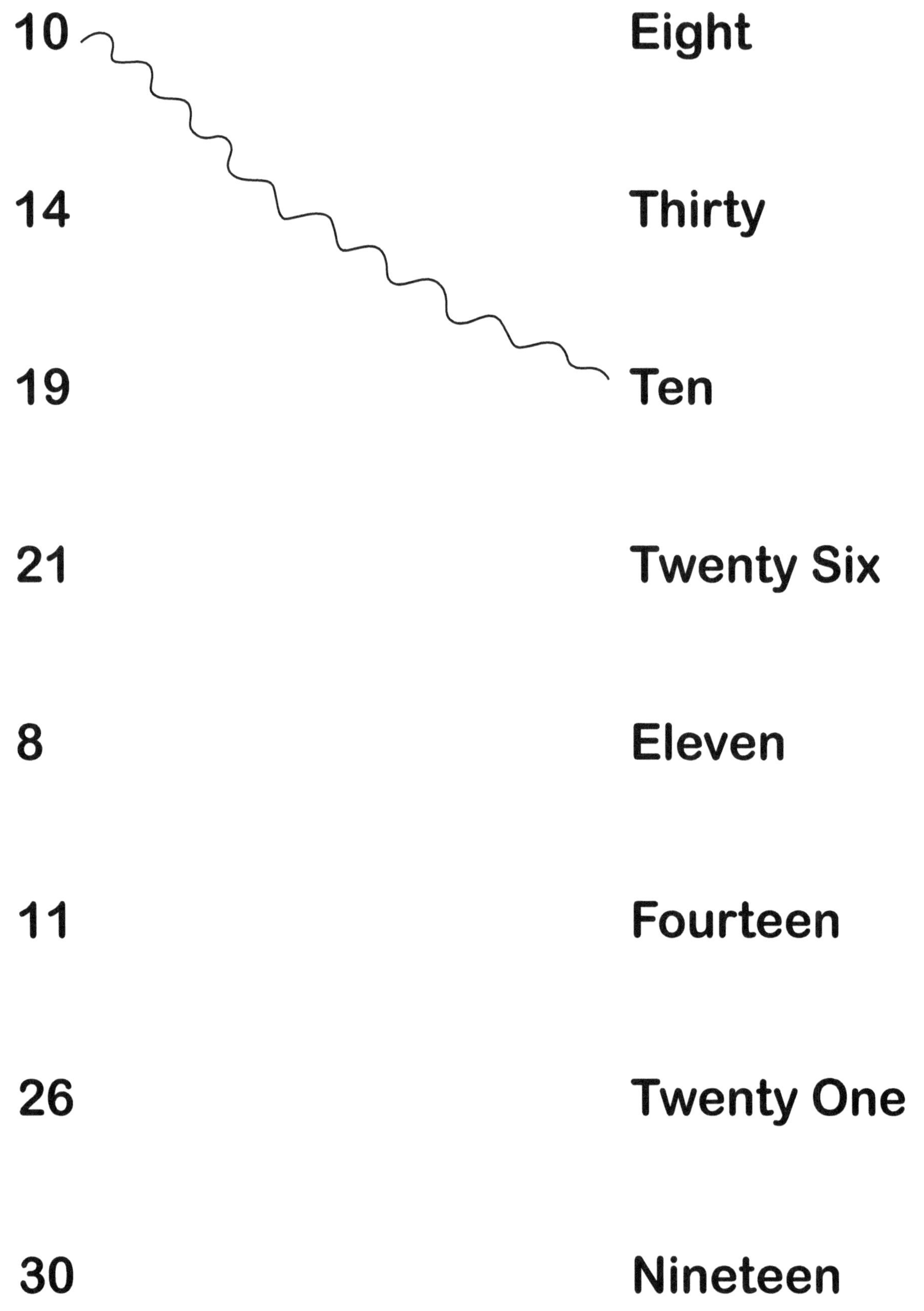

10	**Eight**
14	**Thirty**
19	**Ten**
21	**Twenty Six**
8	**Eleven**
11	**Fourteen**
26	**Twenty One**
30	**Nineteen**

Look at the picture given below. Colour all the objects beginning with letter 'B'.

Complete the word grid after identifying the objects.

Jumbo English Activity-1

mango / watermelon

spoon / fork

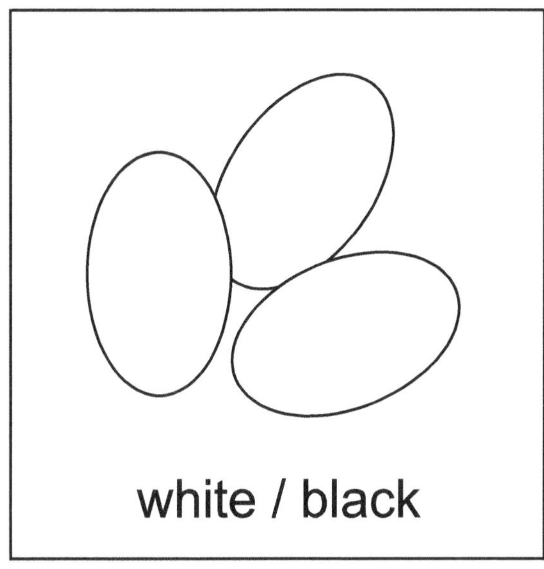

white / black

hot / cold

T-shirt / frock

sofa / table

Unscramble the words.

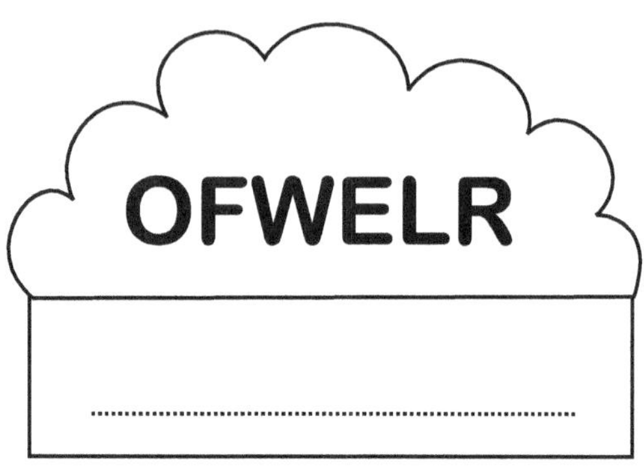

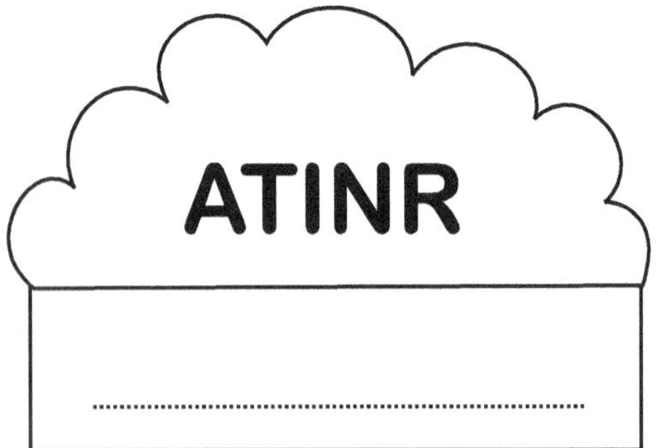

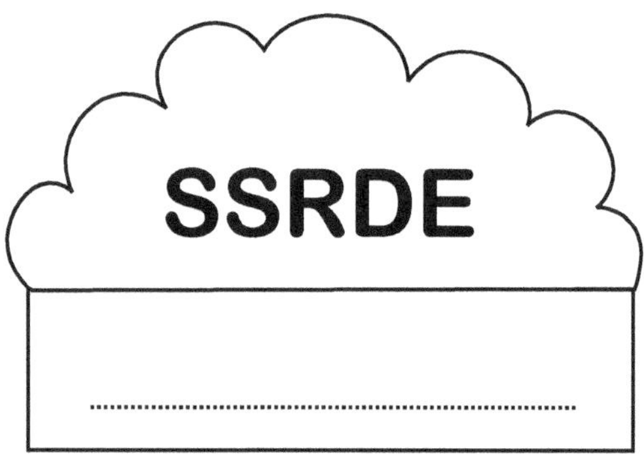

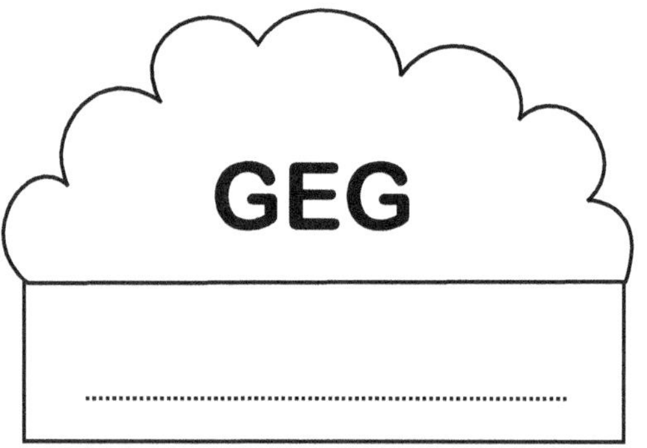

Jumbo English Activity–

Find the names of days of a week in the following grid. Colour them to separate.

B	W	E	D	N	E	S	D	A	Y
R	J	Q	F	L	R	M	Y	N	B
T	H	U	R	S	D	A	Y	A	M
R	N	Z	I	R	I	F	A	C	O
S	A	Q	D	H	Z	J	A	S	N
U	A	T	A	F	P	A	K	U	D
N	G	W	Y	O	E	U	A	G	A
D	T	U	E	S	D	A	Y	A	Y
A	X	M	A	L	M	V	P	T	E
Y	S	A	T	U	R	D	A	Y	X

SUNDAY	THURSDAY
MONDAY	FRIDAY
TUESDAY	SATURDAY
WEDNESDAY	

Colour only those apples that have words with 'a' sound.

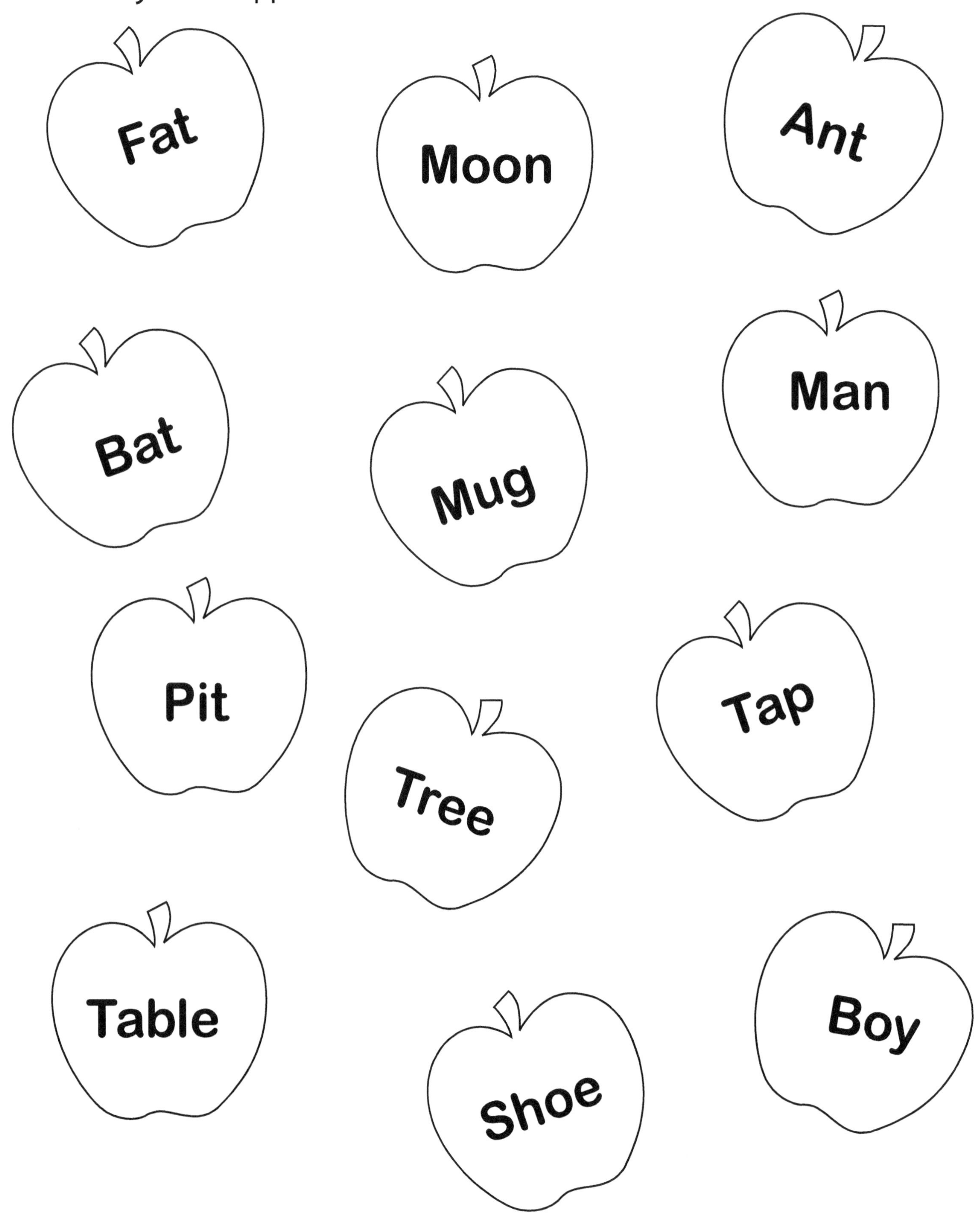

Jumbo English Activity-1

Underline the vowels (a, e, i, o, u) in each word.

Lips	Watch
Apple	Jug
Fruit	Bird
Towel	Sun
Pan	Book
Kite	Chair
Funny	Mouse
Box	Picnic

Colour the things which have letters 'ch' in them.

94

Pussy cat, pussy cat,
where have you been
I've been to London
to visit the Queen.
Pussy cat, pussy cat,
what did you do there?
I frightened a little mouse
under the chair.

been

Queen

1. Nita .... cooking food.

2. They .... going for a picnic.

3. He .... good at playing guitar.

4. Rahul .... singing a song.

5. Saket and Vaibhav .... brothers.

6. It .... my pet dog.

7. Maya .... not at home.

8. All of us .... watching television.

Jumbo English Activity-1

Dear Sarthak,

I'm coming 2 your 

at  o'clock. We'll play 

and then watch 

I'll get some 

and 

My  will come to pick me up

at  o'clock.

Bye,

Ketan

Fill the following crossword puzzle with right words given at the bottom in right boxes.

ACROSS
1. ant
2. rat
3. spider
4. bee

DOWN
1. tortoise
2. beetle

Fill in the blanks with the correct letters given in the central column and link them with pictures.

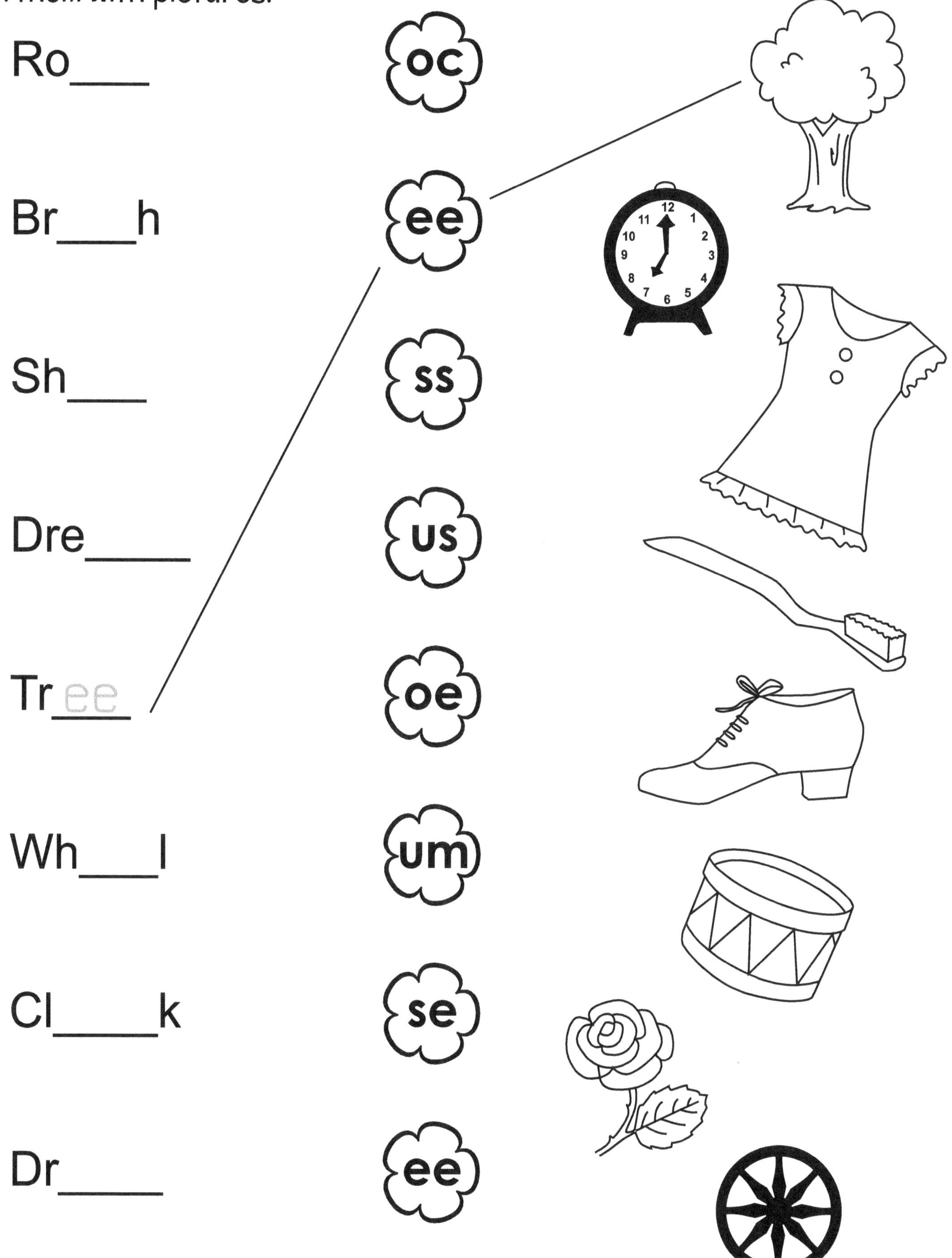

Ro___

Br___h

Sh___

Dre____

Tr_ee_

Wh___l

Cl___k

Dr____

oc

ee

ss

us

oe

um

se

ee

Find out the correct action words for the pictures.

Jumbo English Activity-1

With the letters in the word SPIDERMAN how many words can you make?
An example is given for you to follow.

SPIDERMAN

DREAM   MID

Identify the given objects. We are giving 3 name options for each object. Colour the correct one.

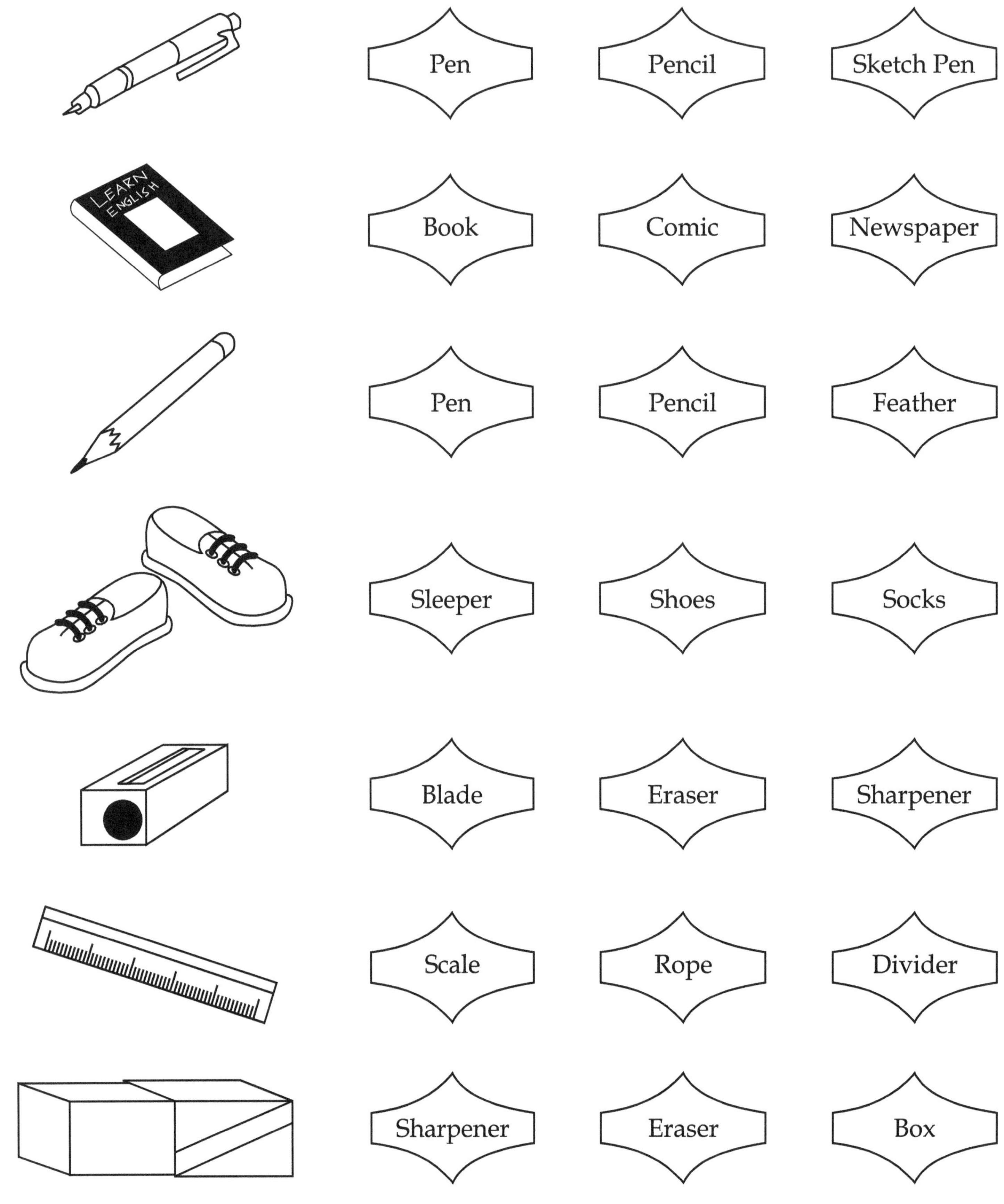

Jumbo English Activity—

Every design stands for a letter. Study the example (School) carefully and write down other words the design clues make.

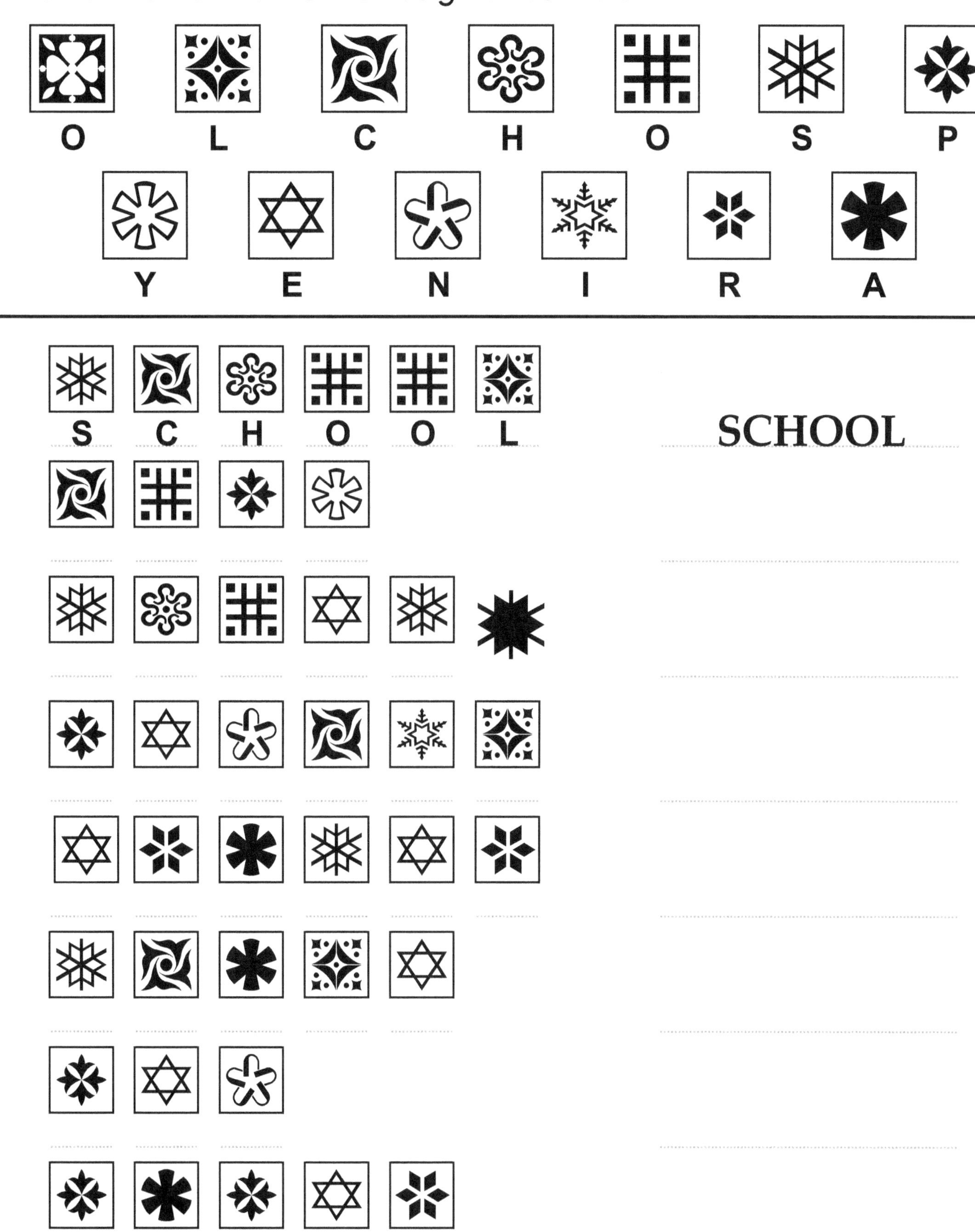

SCHOOL

Name the shapes and colour them differently.

Jumbo English Activity-1

You know your body parts well. See the pictures and write correct answer.

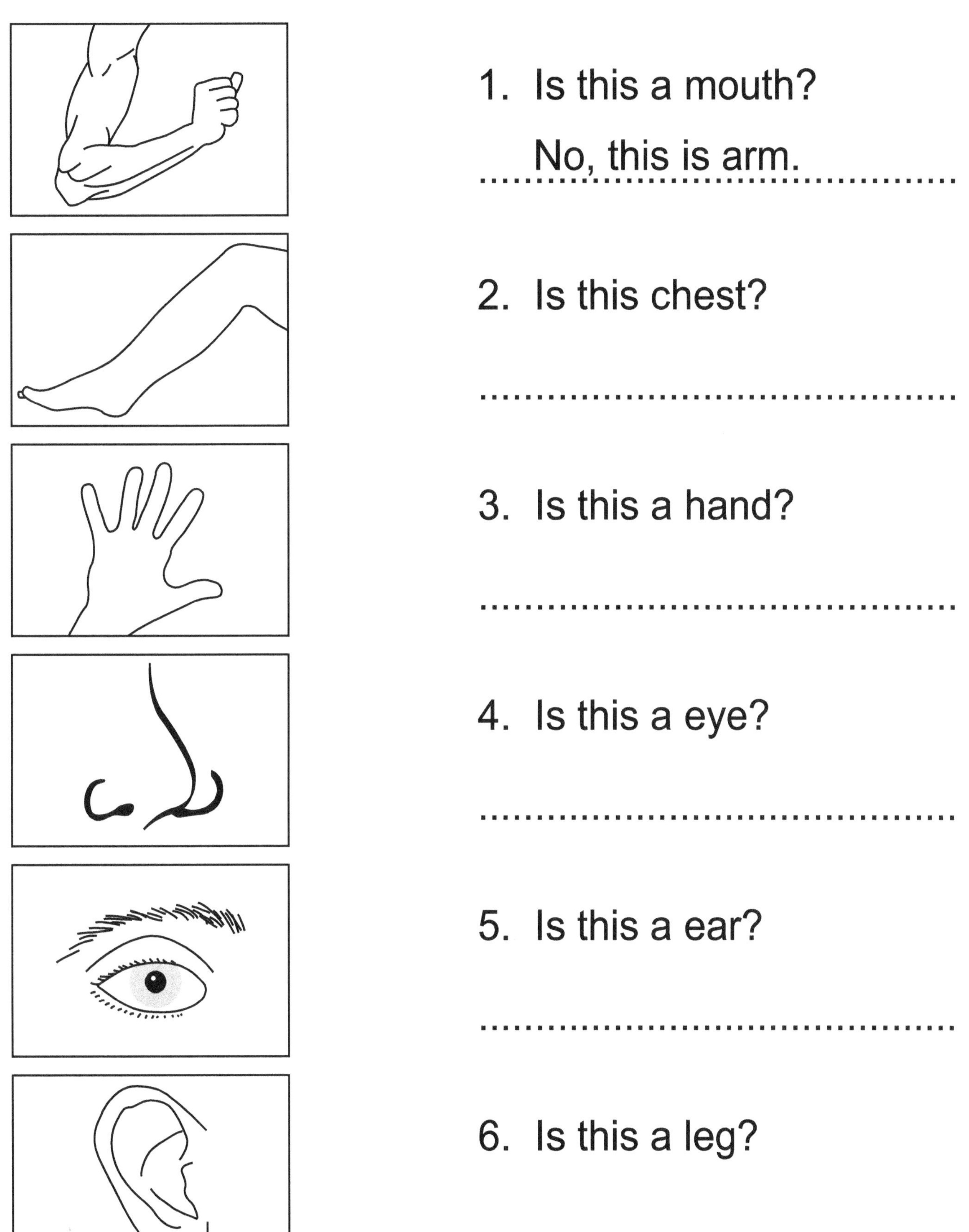

1. Is this a mouth?

......No, this is arm......................

2. Is this chest?

....

3. Is this a hand?

....

4. Is this a eye?

....

5. Is this a ear?

....

6. Is this a leg?

....

With the help of word grid write down the letters in the blank boxes to make a word.

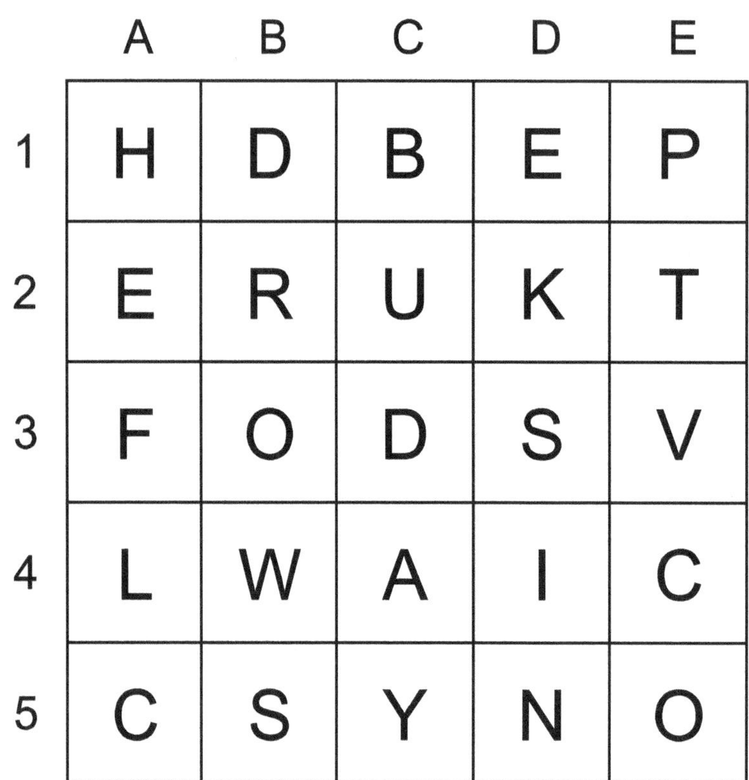

3C 2B 1D 5B 3D

1E 4C 5D

3A 4D 5B 1A

2E 3B 5C

1C 2A 3C

5A 4A 3B 4E 2D

Jumbo English Activity–

Colour the objects that start with the letters FO.

Follow the instructions given on the clouds and make as many words as you can.

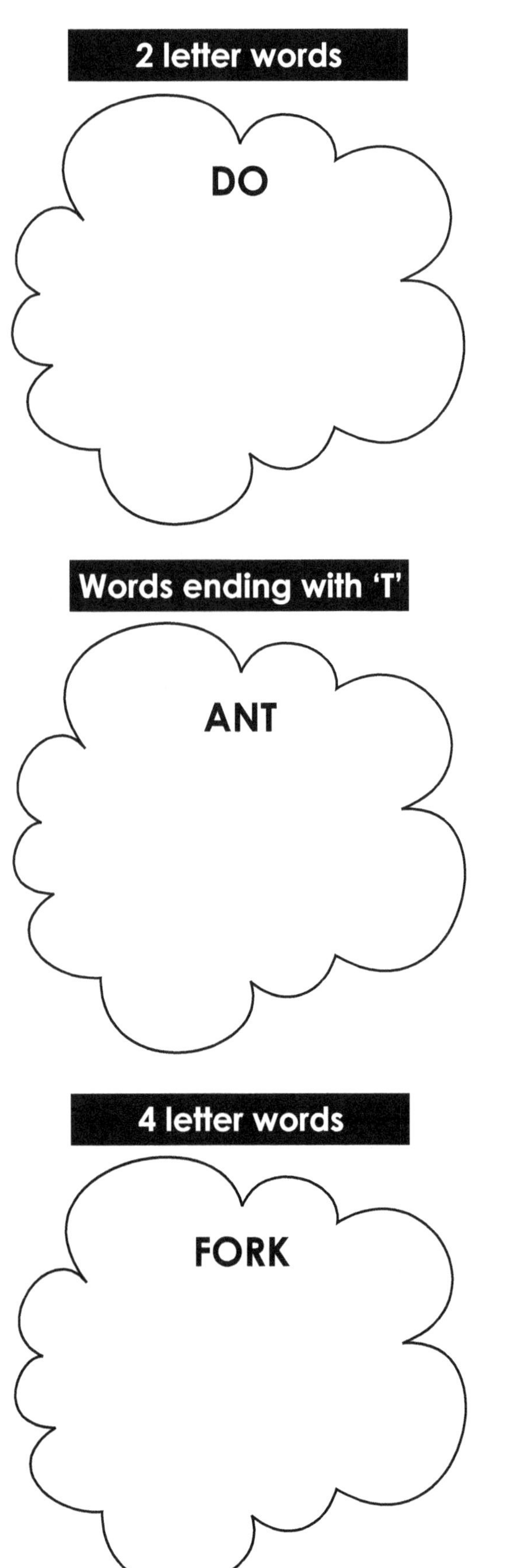

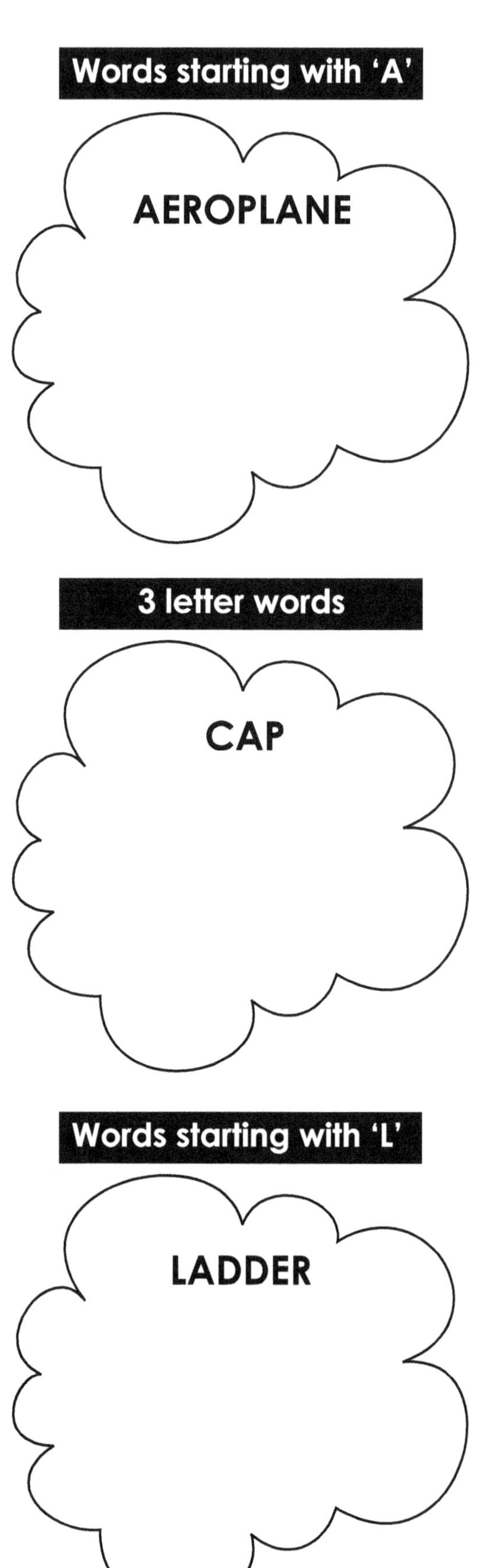

Jumbo English Activity-1

Write the first letter of the word the pictures start with in the wagon wheel.
Assemble the letters to form a new word.

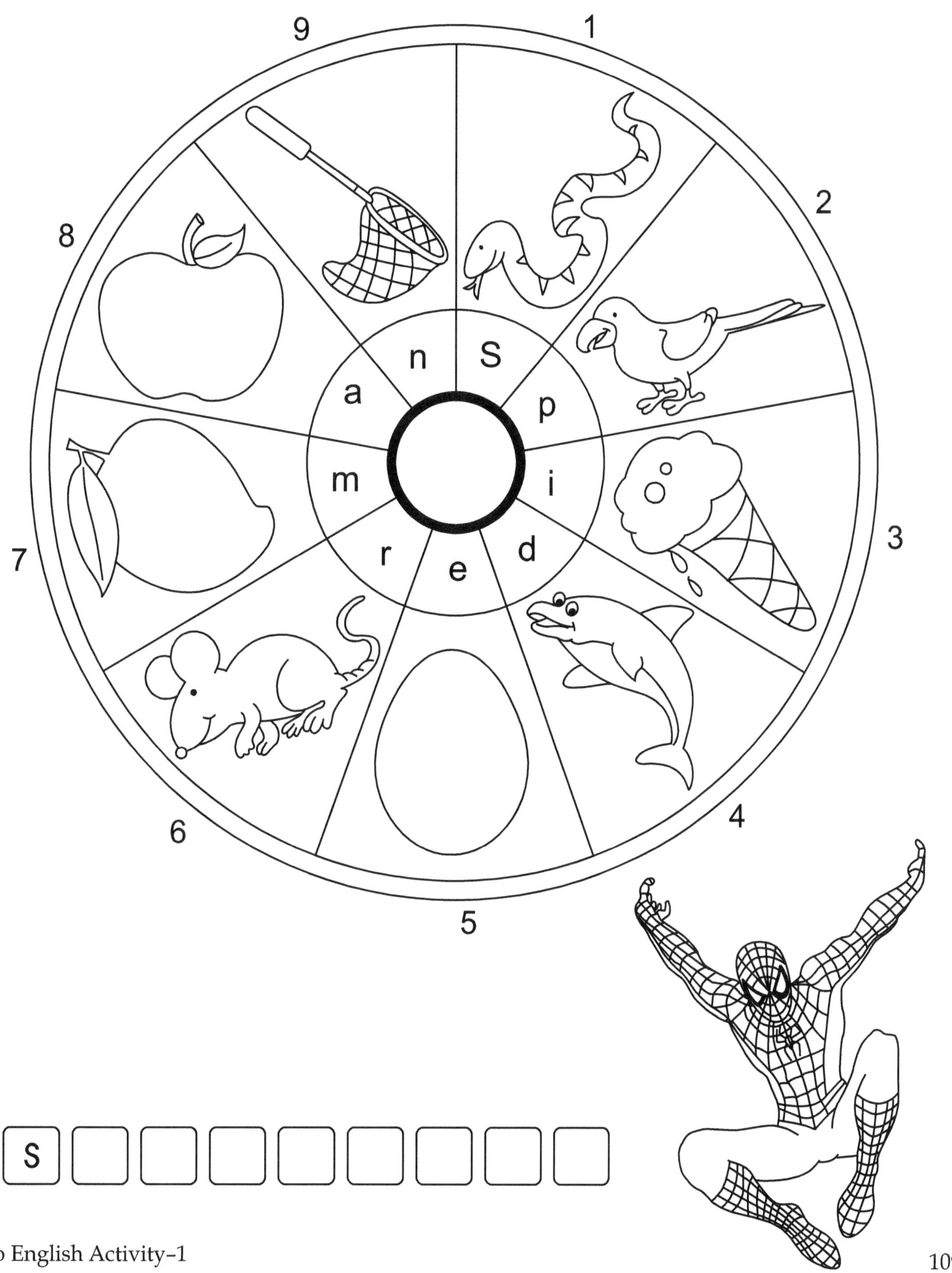

Spell test! Tick (✓) mark the correct spelling for the given pictures.

☐ Bat
☐ Bet

☐ Dolphin
☐ Dolpin

☐ Duck
☐ Dack

☐ Butterfli
☐ Butterfly

☐ Clock
☐ Cloak

☐ Girafe
☐ Giraffe

☐ Yacht
☐ Yact

☐ Rabbit
☐ Rabit

☐ King
☐ Kinge

  Jumbo English Activity–

Unscramble the word to see where the boy is taking his dog to. And colour the picture.

C O R O T D

D ☐ ☐ ☐ ☐ R

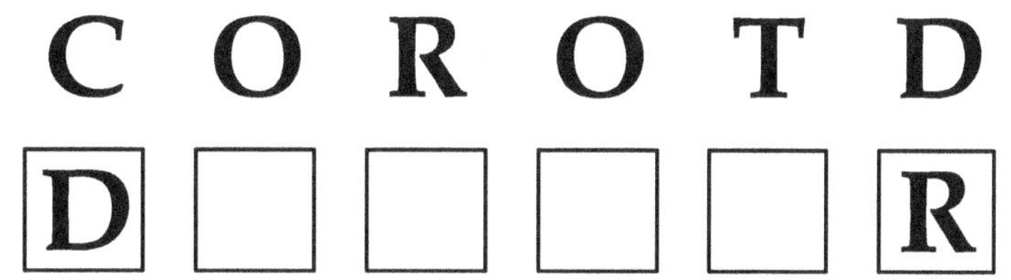

Sanjeev sir is telling opposites. He wants you to colour the smaller objects and name them.

Find the names of the pictured objects in the letter parades given below.

P F C (R) (A) A O (T) S E

S S M N A T K S E Q

M F D A O N O S R D

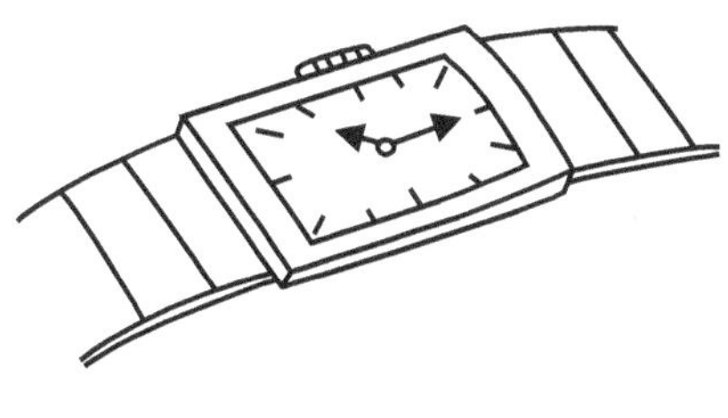

B W T A O T W C I H

F B O L P A E J L L

T P H R O A E S Y E

Jumbo English Activity–

Find a way to come out of maze. You have to go through all the 26 alphabet in this process.

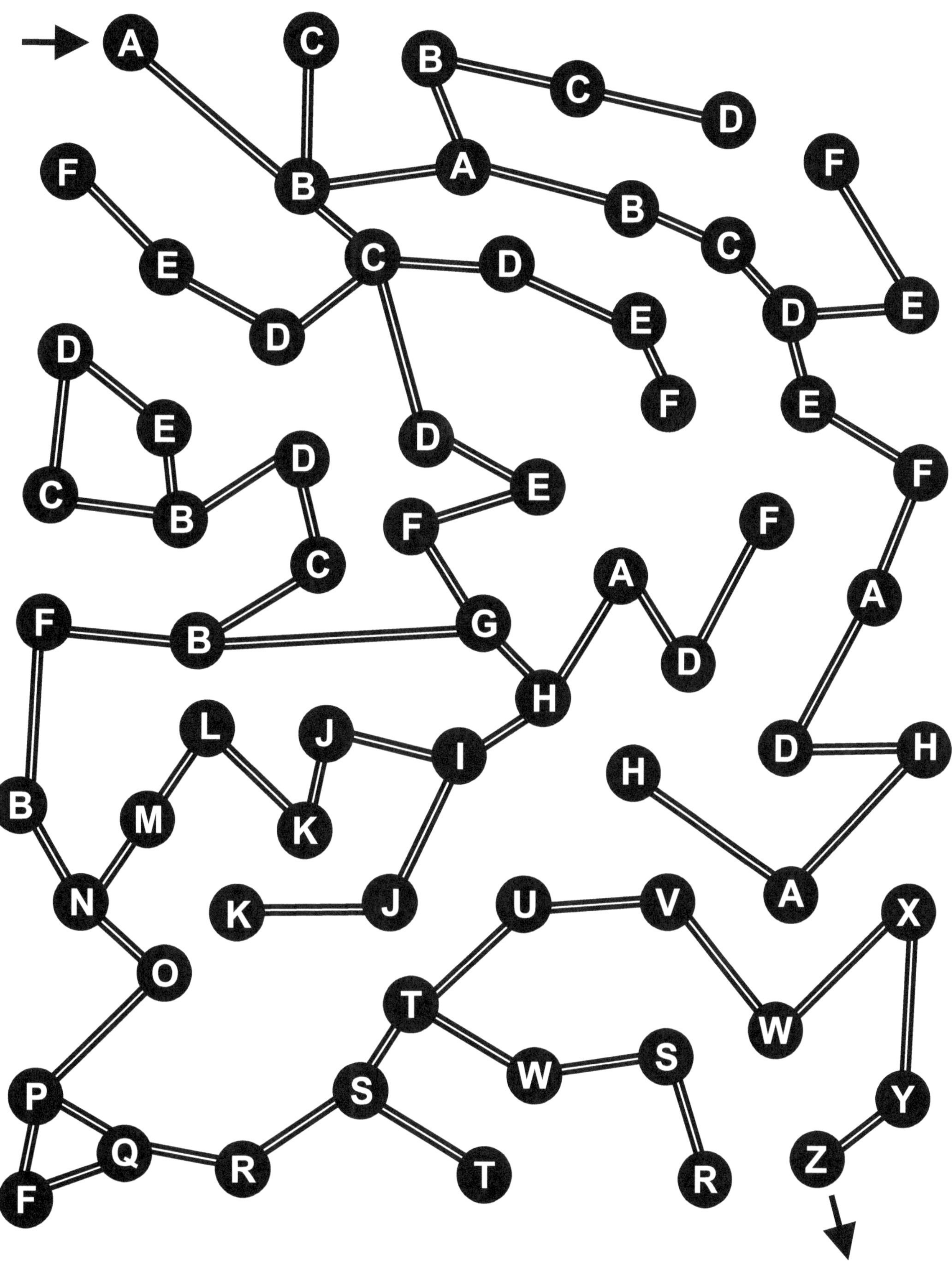

Mistakenly Minni has mixed all the things. Can you help her sort them apart?

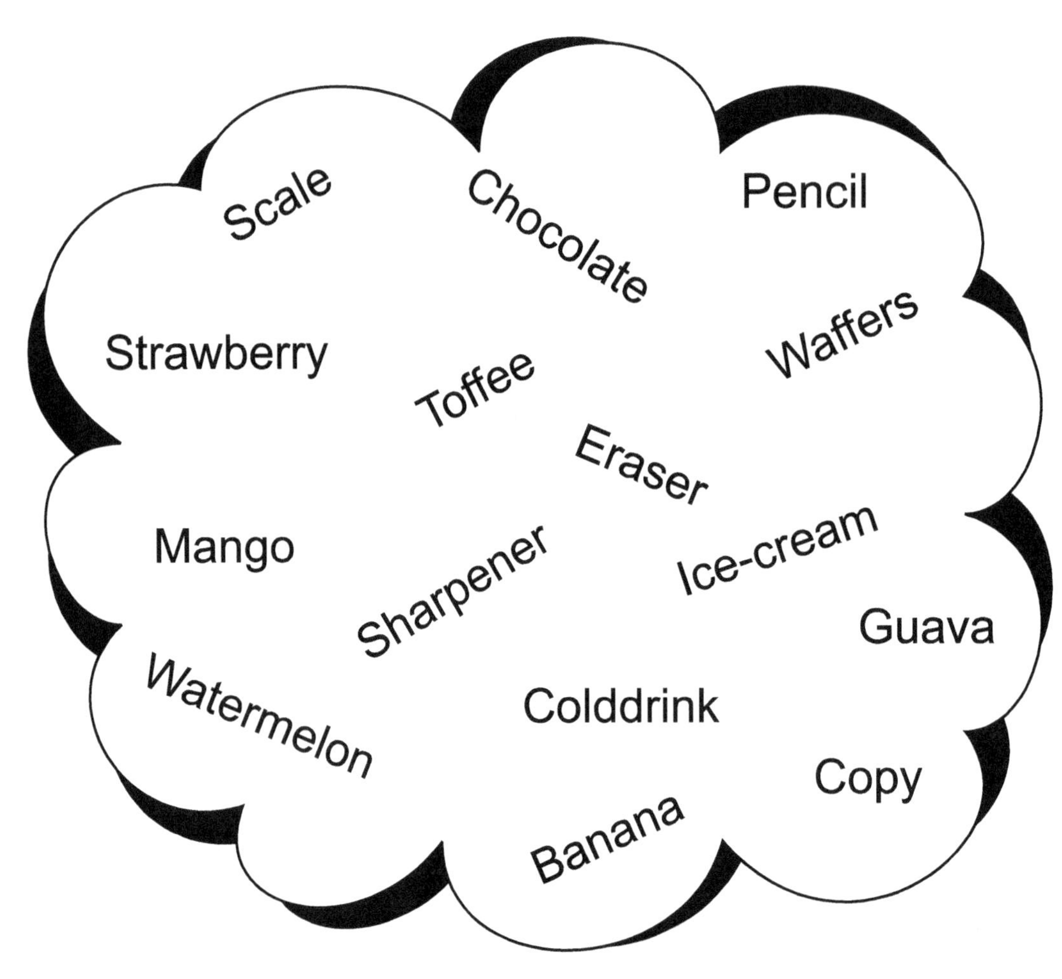

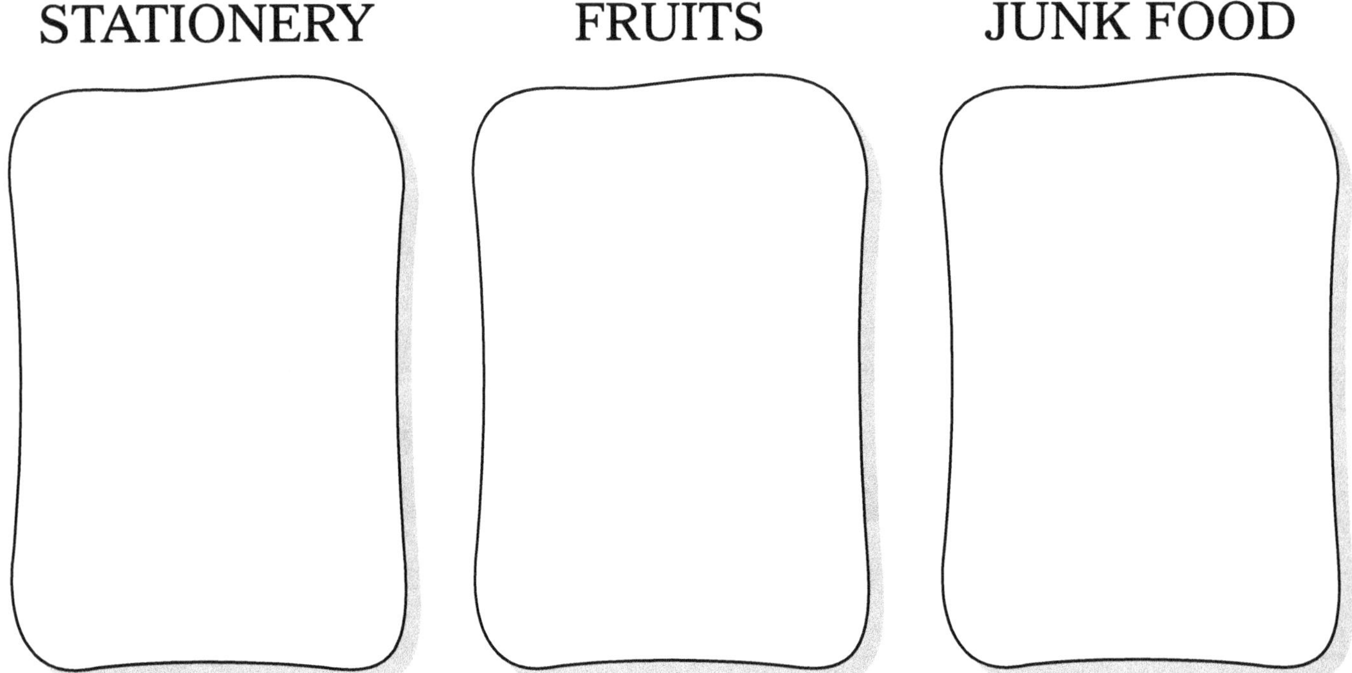

STATIONERY	FRUITS	JUNK FOOD

Use your mind and tell which colour belongs to which object.

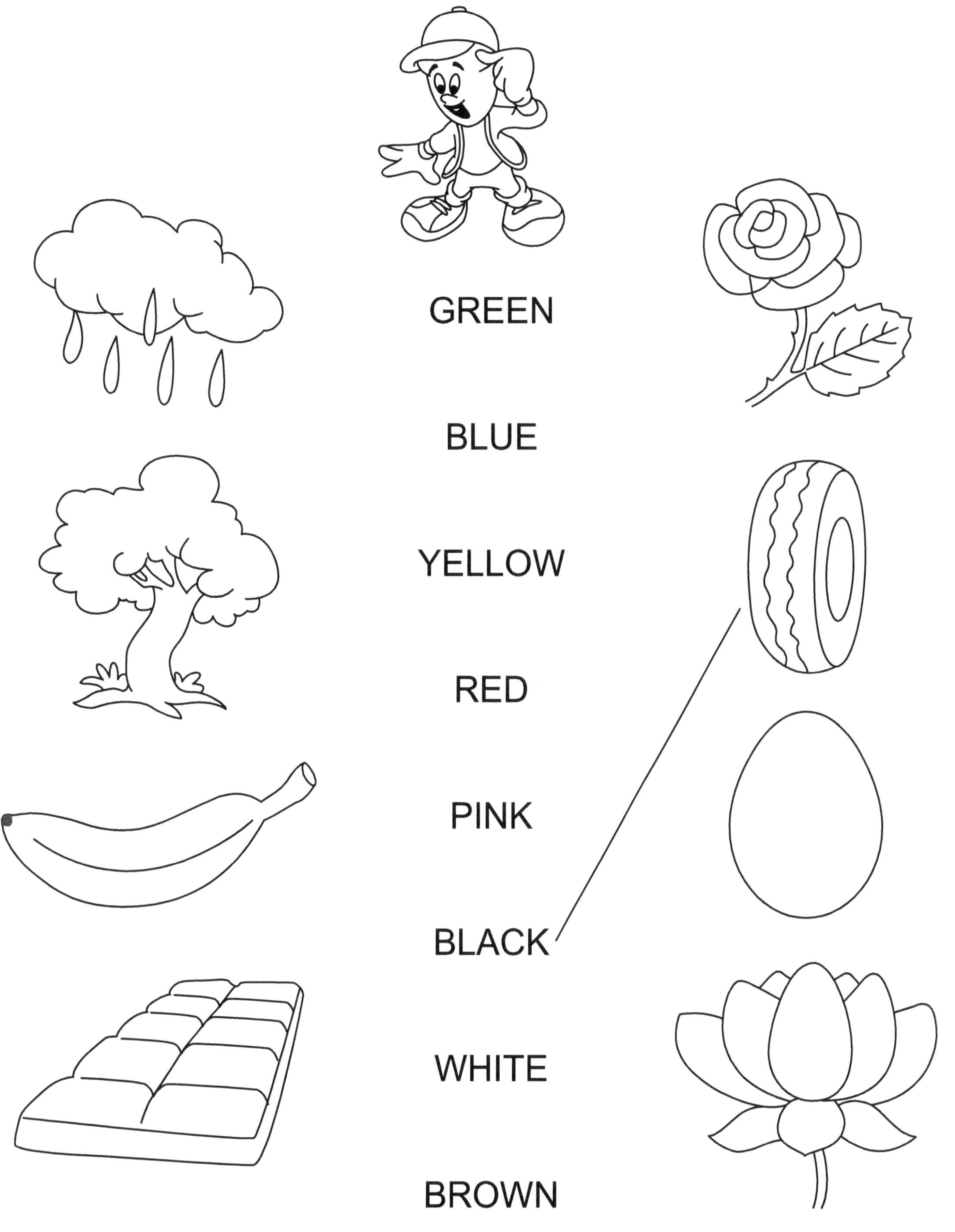

(1) What is the girl on the left is carrying? ....

(2) What does the boy hold in his hand? ....

(3) What is the mother pushing? ....

(4) Where are the three appear to be? ....

(5) Who is the youngest of the three? ....

Clue—Shopping Mall, Trollcy, Ice cream, Box, Boy

Jumbo English Activity–

Unscramble the words given below to make meaningful names of the items.

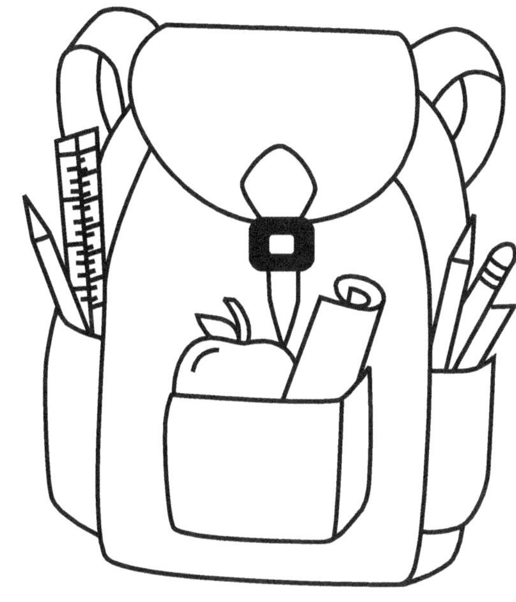

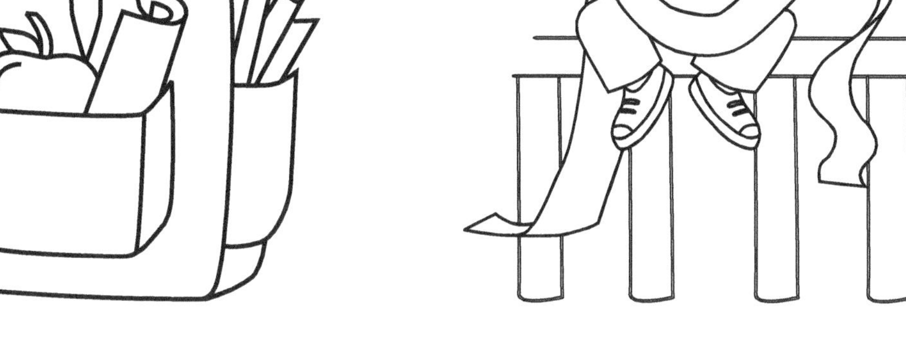

LASEC   ______________

RADIY   ______________

RAEESR   ______________

NCPELI   ______________

HAPRERSNE   ______________

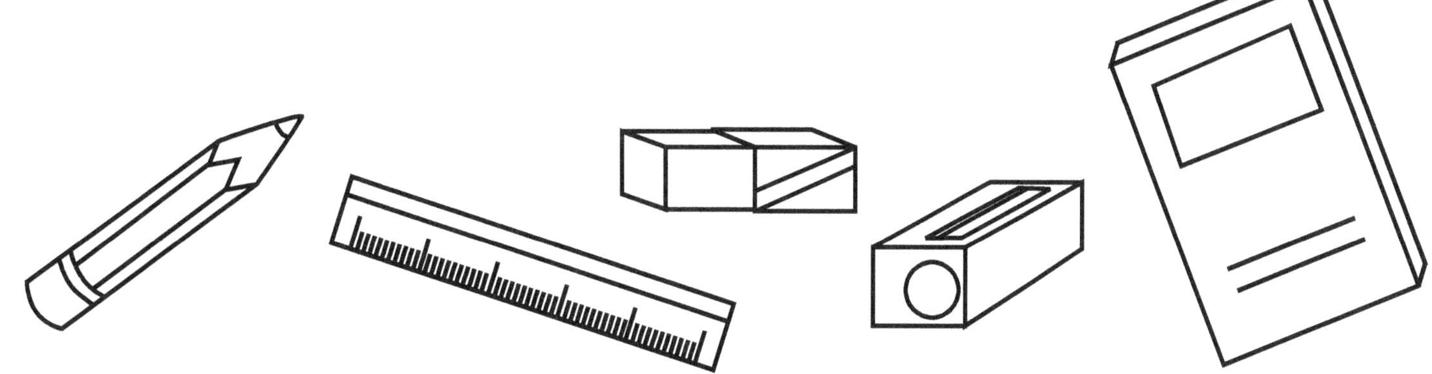

Look at the pictures given below and fill in the blanks.

1. Rita is reading a ....

2. He is playing ....

3. The dog is lapping ....

4. Sohan is eating ....

5. Rohan is watching ....

6. Vicky is .... fast.

Jumbo English Activity-1

Fill in the blanks with the correct words for the genders or young one of the animals.

Dog   Bitch   Puppy   Cow   Ox   Calf   Sheep   Ewe
Lamb   Cock   Hen   Chick   Tom   Cat   Kitten

Male	Female	Babies

Dog	Bitch	Puppy

In the crossword find out the animal names and colour them.

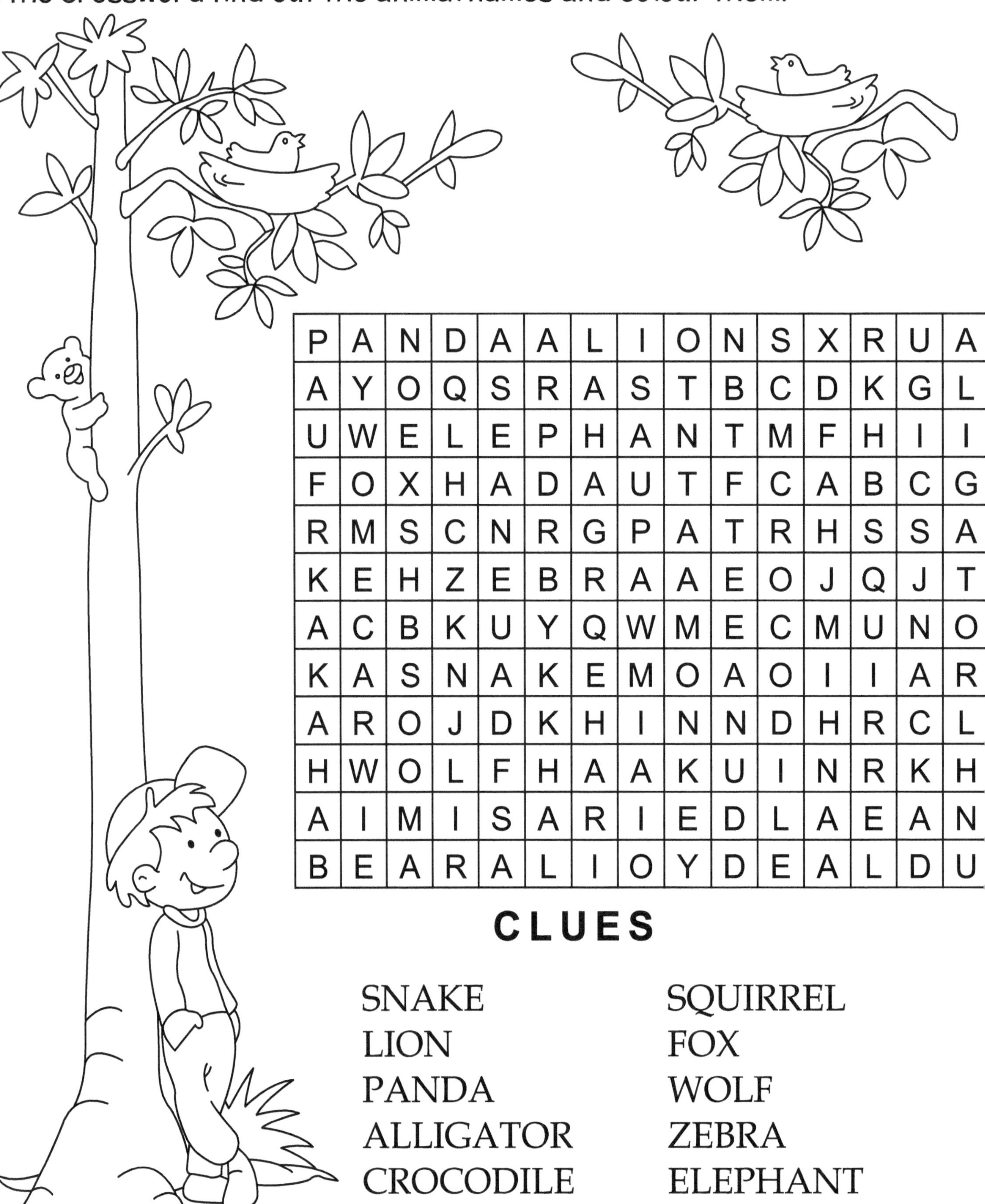

P	A	N	D	A	A	L	I	O	N	S	X	R	U	A
A	Y	O	Q	S	R	A	S	T	B	C	D	K	G	L
U	W	E	L	E	P	H	A	N	T	M	F	H	I	I
F	O	X	H	A	D	A	U	T	F	C	A	B	C	G
R	M	S	C	N	R	G	P	A	T	R	H	S	S	A
K	E	H	Z	E	B	R	A	A	E	O	J	Q	J	T
A	C	B	K	U	Y	Q	W	M	E	C	M	U	N	O
K	A	S	N	A	K	E	M	O	A	O	I	I	A	R
A	R	O	J	D	K	H	I	N	N	D	H	R	C	L
H	W	O	L	F	H	A	A	K	U	I	N	R	K	H
A	I	M	I	S	A	R	I	E	D	L	A	E	A	N
B	E	A	R	A	L	I	O	Y	D	E	A	L	D	U

CLUES

SNAKE   SQUIRREL

LION   FOX

PANDA   WOLF

ALLIGATOR   ZEBRA

CROCODILE   ELEPHANT

BEAR   MONKEY

Jumbo English Activity–

Match and colour the picture as indicated.

Trees are GREEN

Clouds are BLUE

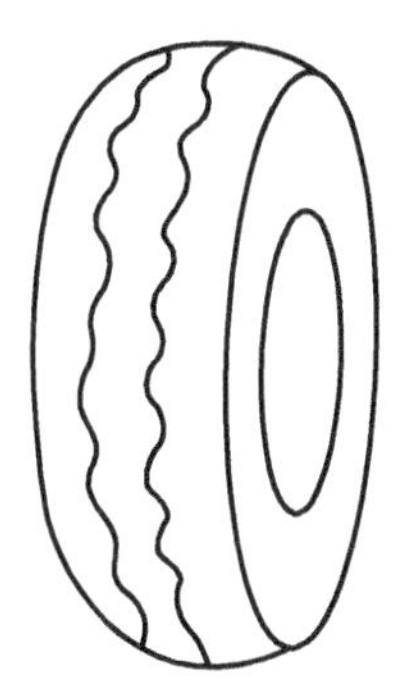

Banana is YELLOW

Roses are RED

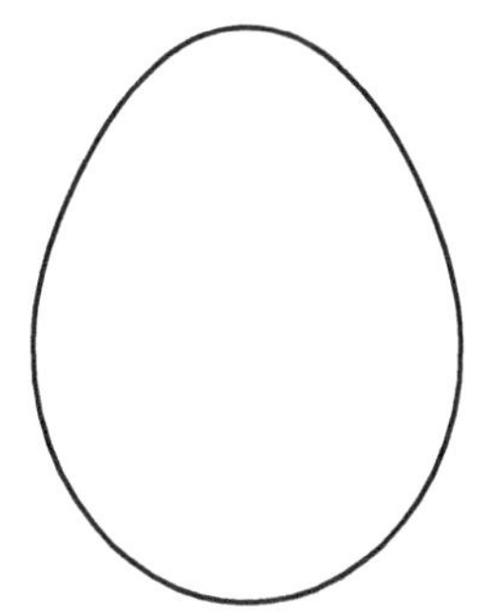

Lotus is PINK

Tyre is BLACK

Egg is WHITE

Chocolate is BROWN

Write the name of what each picture shows. Colour those pictures which start with letter B.

1. 

2. 

3. 

4. 

5. 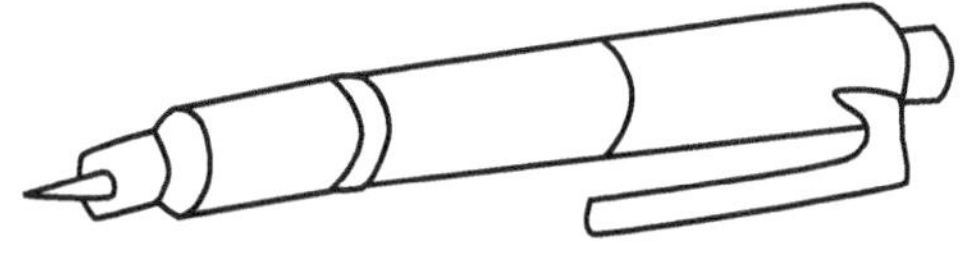

6. 

7. 

8. 

9. 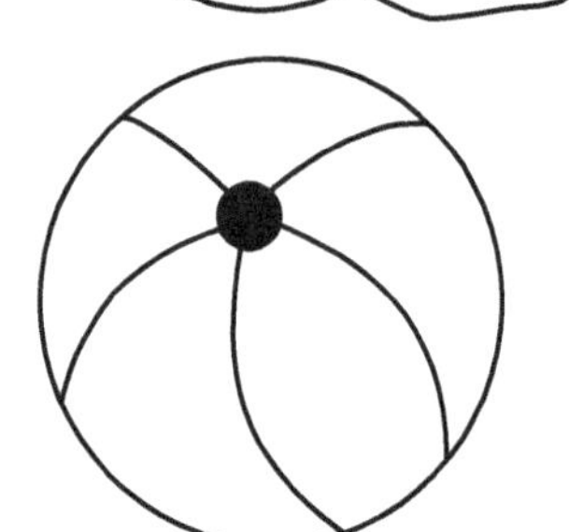

10. 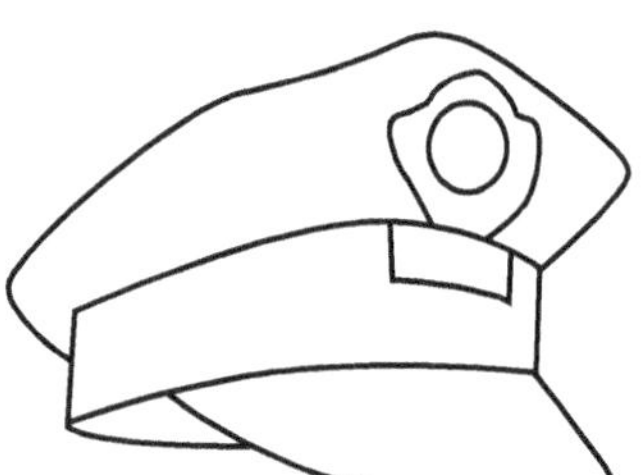

11. 

12. 

Jumbo English Activity-1

Match the pictures of your body parts with correct words.

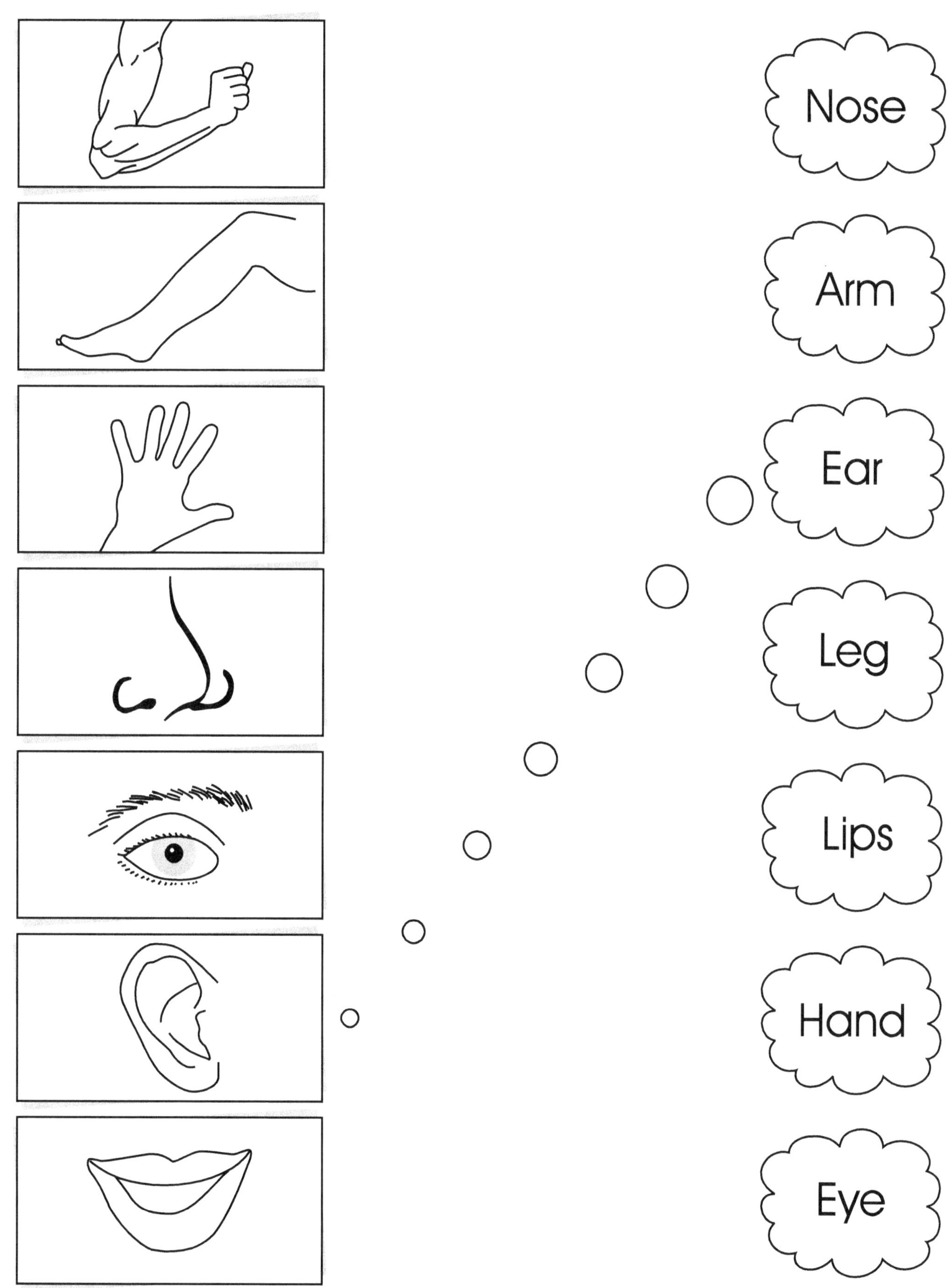

Bholu elephant is holding some words that need letters WH or CH to complete them. Write the correct pair to make each word.

Jumbo English Activity-

Write the numbers in Roman and in words.

20	XX	Twenty
11		
17		
29		
5		
21		
5		
19		
16		
22		
7		
9		

Try to make as many words from the letters of the given word in each box.

CHILDREN

SPIDERMAN

CHRISTMAS

CROCODILE

ELEPHANT

POMEGRANATE

Jumbo English Activity-1

www.ingramcontent.com/pod-product-compliance
Lightning Source LLC
LaVergne TN
LVHW060407200726
843506LV00007B/390